The Culture of Heaven
and The Destiny of Peoples

The Culture of Heaven
And
The Destiny of Peoples

David A. Melander
March 2019

XULON PRESS

Xulon Press
2301 Lucien Way #415
Maitland, FL 32751
407.339.4217
www.xulonpress.com

© 2019 by David A. Melander

All rights reserved solely by the author. The author guarantees all contents are original and do not infringe upon the legal rights of any other person or work. No part of this book may be reproduced in any form without the permission of the author. The views expressed in this book are not necessarily those of the publisher.

Scripture quotations taken from the New American Standard Bible (NASB). Copyright © 1960, 1962, 1963, 1968, 1971, 1972, 1973, 1975, 1977, 1995 by The Lockman Foundation. Used by permission. All rights reserved.

Printed in the United States of America.

ISBN-13: 9781545679364

Table of Contents

Introduction xiii
Chapter 1: Jesus Shares His Birthright 1
Chapter 2: The Culture of Heaven 10
Chapter 3: Kingdom Family 26
Chapter 4: Father's Movement 34
Chapter 5: The Destiny of Peoples 48
Chapter 6: Glory 67
Chapter 7: Stirring the Passions of
          the Almighty 84
Chapter 8: Removing a Heart of Stone and
          of Religion 97
Chapter 9: A Cleansing from Love Growing Cold 111
Chapter 10: God's Fame in the World, Daniel
           and Joseph 125
Chapter 11: Loving and Embracing All that
           He Loves 145
Afterword 153
About the author 157

The vision to "make the world a better place" sounds noble; it's been inspiring humans to noble aspirations since Plato's Republic. "Come on people, let's fix the world!" Sadly, all our efforts at Utopia end as sputtering failures – at best – and totalitarian tyrannies – at worst. Even Christians have at times traded the regenerative power of the Gospel for the niceties of personal and social improvement. But there's only one true revolution – the actual invasion of Heaven to earth! In his book *The Culture of Heaven* David Melander highlights this revolution – God's Kingdom here and now on earth. Only Jesus' genuine reign delivers restorative power and when His "culture of heaven" prevails, individuals, families, cultures and nations are not "conquered" or subdued but are liberated to fulfill their destiny. I heartily recommend *The Culture of Heaven* as a grounding vision, a Biblical mandate, and a model and inspiration for what is possible (and already happening) on earth when Heaven and Heaven's King invades!

- Mark Herringshaw, Ph.D., Former Pastor,
Board Chair of YWAM Associates,

David A. Melander

> and currently Partner in GiANT Worldwide,
> a global leadership consultancy, author

This is like a Kingdom manual for transformation for whole cities and regions! Not only that, but **how** you the reader can begin to have the Kingdom mindsets and practical outworkings to be a part of bringing that transformation. Read this, hear the modern day testimonies of Jesus in action through his people, rise as a son or daughter of His and apply it into your life - you can and shall make a difference for the King!

- Andy Piggott, Senior Leader, Bethel New Zealand

In his book, *The Culture of Heaven*, David Melander makes extensive use of the Word of God. One of my favorite Scriptures is "…your words came, I ate them; they were my joy and my heart's delight" (Jeremiah 15:16). It is obvious that David and I are "cut from the same cloth"—God uses the Scriptures to speak to us. David highlights the importance of sons and daughters of God and says, "creation eagerly waits for" them (Romans 8:19).

I recommend this book to all those seeking to have confidence that they are operating in the will of God (1 John 5:14-15).

The Culture of Heaven And The Destiny of Peoples

- Rick Heeren, Vice President, Transform Our World

Believers are seated with Christ in heavenly places and therefore living in a different culture. This book calls us into that culture and demonstrates its life and function in the world. David is a listener who obeys the promptings of the Holy Spirit. He has keen insight into the Word of God, the mind of the Spirit, and our destiny in Christ. Heaven's culture gives us a point of view by which we are to regard everyone and everything. This book calls forth a destiny for us based on biblical revelation and perspective from the Spirit of God.

- Greg Berglund, M.D., M. Div., author of *This Mountain* and *Using Jesus Name*

I have known David for years and I have watched him build the Kingdom wherever he is. David's heart is passionate about releasing true sons and daughters in this world. His unique set of giftings will equip and empower you. I am grateful that he wrote this book from a place as a son, sharing from his heart.

- Alisha Siemens, ARISE! Women's Ministries, Founder and CEO Shema Global, an anti-trafficking clothing line

David Melander served International Lutheran Renewal for decades, inspiring people to step into the experience of the Holy Spirit. His book on *The Culture of Heaven* is a compelling vision for what Jesus is speaking to his church in this hour. His stories (and he has lots of them) will grab your attention and touch your heart. Get ready.

- Paul Anderson, Director, Harvest Communities, Director, International Lutheran Renewal

If you have ever said, "I desire to be close to God", then Dave Melander's book is your road map to that end, *The Culture of Heaven and the Destiny of Peoples*. The heart of moving close to Our Father is rooted in Rom 8:19 and to begin a constant dialogue with Him. Reading this work will demonstrate how this happens in your life. Dave Melander is a son who speaks to our Lord and hears His voice. It has helped me immensely to understand the language of heaven.

- Bob Cottingham, Senior Pastor, North Heights Lutheran Church (retired), Lutheran World Relief, Director for Africa

Introduction

My flight was coming into Amsterdam, connecting to Frankfurt. I travel a lot for business. I was coming to a series of business meetings and to attend a large trade show in Hamburg, Germany. On the way I was planning to travel through Leipzig to see some people who had become very dear to me. They were part of a historic church there that had experienced amazing transformation when the Holy Spirit visited them. The place was packed with young people who were just coming into fellowship with Jesus.

As my plane was landing, I was thinking about changing my flight, to go directly to Leipzig from Amsterdam instead of flying to Frankfurt and taking the train from there. That was only logical. It would save hours of travel. Unfortunately, I felt a sense of "self-importance" because of my role in business. But I sensed the dear Lord Jesus tell me, "don't change your travel plans, I have someone for you to meet". I felt that he had "appointed" me to say something for him to someone. So I just left my plans as is. That meant, it turns out, that I would take *3 trains* on the way and I was a little unhappy to learn that. But I trusted that he knows best, because, well, he actually *does* know best.

I was excited on the first train to meet the person I was appointed to meet. I talked to a lot of people but nothing exceptionally supernatural happened. Same with the second train. So many interesting, nice people! By the third train I was getting tired and not in the best mood. I forgot I was on a mission altogether. At some point on the route I started having a very interesting conversation with a very educated woman about geo-politics and natural capital, I heard the whisper of Holy Spirit. I turned my heart to listen and I heard, "this is the person I want you to meet". When I opened my heart to hear his heart I saw her life story in a flash. I saw something of Father's beautiful intention for her life. I saw the day her mother told her father that she was pregnant. I saw her father very angry and I saw him walk out forever. Then I did something wise and I am lucky because I am not always as spiritual as I should be. That is, I asked the Lord what he wanted to do with all that.

Everyone knows that Jesus is very wise. But in this situation I could really see this in living color. He showed me how to approach the situation with this woman I had just met. I know that sometimes when people have revelations they can "use" the information, as a form of power over people. But I do not see that in Jesus. In his wisdom he reminded me that when I had last been in Leipzig I had ministered to someone named Antje whose life story was very similar to the woman sitting across from me. In the ministry time with Antje, Father had met her in a dramatic and wonderful way. Father had really revealed himself personally, sweetly, deeply. And so I asked my fellow trainmate if I could change the subject to something personal and she agreed. And I shared Antje's story and how she met Father. Now I knew my trainmate was not yet a Jesus-person, that she was somewhat cynical about "religion". But as I shared Antje's story my friend in the train had tears running down her cheeks, profusely. At one point she asked me, with her voice quavering, "why did you share that with me?" And I felt the softness in Father's heart well up inside me and I said, "because I know it's also your story".

We talked then for a couple of hours about Father and how he has known her from the very beginning, how she is constantly on his mind. I shared how he had shown me his thoughts toward her along the path of her life. It melted her heart toward Abba and she wanted to come to know him. She said, "if you had asked me even an hour ago if I believed in God I would have said 'no' but now it is undeniable how real and present he is." She met her Father.

The whole thing was beautiful. I felt beautiful myself. I felt the pleasure of Abba going through me.

I think this experience illustrates some of what I want to share in this book. The message is simple in a way, that our destiny is in another country and another culture. We are going to live there forever, beautifully. Yet, to some degree, I may suggest that some of us may experience some culture shock in that event. How we live now, how we strive in our lives toward security, material goods, and reputation will really all pass away. We also hold very tightly to our own ideas and opinions, some of which are not like heaven at all. Some of these opinions are from hurt, weakness, self-protection or even human prejudice. And some of these things need to be "plowed up" and displaced by eternal culture that flows from the heart and mind of God.

I am offering my perspective on the culture of heaven as an invitation to start the process of "enculturation" toward that eternal home and country. There is good reason that we should become deeply saturated with heaven's culture now, even while we are still waiting for it. As we start to share heaven's perspective, it's way of thinking, it's attitudes, we change to be more like Jesus and Father. It beautifies us.

As we become enculturated to heaven's mindset, we minister to other people out of a new place, with nothing to gain but joy and fellowship. We become of no reputation and we have no need for it with one exception. That is, we love it when Jesus speaks our name to our Father, the Father who loves us before we even do a thing. As we seek to enter into fellowship with our Father as beloved children, we begin to know his mind and heart. He shares that with us. This puts us in a place where ministry is amplified supernaturally. Spiritual gifts of all sorts begin to come out through us as we have a new priority, all the things that are on our Father's heart.

So becoming enculturated in heaven's culture is good for us and for those around us, especially for people who need to hear something from the heart of heaven, from the deep treasures in the heart of Father for everyone.

One of the verses from the Bible that I really love, from my heart, is Col 3:1, 2 – "Therefore if you have been raised up with Christ, keep seeking the things above, where Christ is, seated at the right hand of God. Set your mind on the things above, not on the things that are on earth."

This book is my sincere effort to share with you some of what I am learning along the way of the culture of heaven, the mind of God, and the destiny of the families and clans of people God created.

Chapter 1

Jesus Shares His Birthright

"Behold I make all things new" (Rev 21:5)

Father is making a new heaven and a new earth. He is making people ready for this place by revealing to them that they are his sons and daughters. This revelation is quietly shaking the creation.

> Rom 8:19 reads, "For the anxious longing of the creation waits eagerly for the revealing of the sons of God. For the creation was subjected to futility, not willingly, but because of Him who subjected it, in hope that the creation itself also will be set free from its slavery to corruption into the freedom of the glory of the children of God. For we know that the

> whole creation groans and suffers the
> pains of childbirth together until now."

What Jesus is doing is beyond measure in its scale. Not only will he, Father, and Holy Spirit bring forward a new heaven and new earth but all of human history, human authority, and human experience will be summed up in Jesus himself (Eph 1:10) as he brings all things to perfect justice (Isa 42:1-4, Matt 12:18-21). He is truly making all things new. We know that this culminates in his return but it is manifesting now in the children who are experiencing sonship and daughterhood as they walk, even in this age. This verse in Romans tells us one aspect of the mission of Jesus, to manifest his glory in the earth by revealing children who walk in joyful freedom. They walk in freedom because they are deeply baptized in love, they are secure in their Daddy's love, and his fragrance manifests where they go. As we begin to live in sonship and freedom, the sons of God become manifest or revealed. The result is the glory of the Lord begins to fill his creation (Hab 2:14, Eph 1:23, Isa 11:9).

Jesus told us something understated but astounding. He said, "do not be afraid, little flock, for your Father has chosen gladly to give you the kingdom" (Luke 12:32). I am thrilled by this statement, mostly how joyful and happy Father is in giving us the eternal treasures of his kingdom.

How great it is that he does this gladly. Jesus showed how true this is by how constantly he was filled with joy in doing Father's work. His intention is clear, that we enter into a cycle of joy in fellowship with Father that results in works borne of joy that please the Father. This thrills Father because the works we do this way are ones of sheer beauty, manifesting the real heart of Father on the earth, just as Jesus did everywhere he went. It creates mutual gladness between us and our Abba.

The best remedy for pride is joyful, childlike connection and fellowship with Father, Jesus, and Holy Spirit. There is no pride there because it is displaced by joy.

Father loves to share his secrets with people. It is a path of fellowship with him. When we learn his secrets in the living context of his heart and his desires we can be somewhat immune to pride. This is because what we see in the heart of Father gently confronts our pride as his beauty stands in contrast to the thinking of this world. We become like him as we see him as he is (1 John 3:2). The joyful experience of sharing his heart is one of seeing beauty, sharing beauty, and becoming beauty. When this happens, there is no room for pride because there is no "spiritual achievement" in the process, there is no "effort" other than seeking him. There is no comparison with other people and no competition. His secrets are freely given to us just in joyful fellowship - and given to us to share, just as he shares. Jesus modelled this constantly and prayed that we would find this path of joy. John 15:11 says, "These things I have spoken to you so that My joy may be in you, and that your joy may be made full". Similarly, John 16:24 says, "Until now you have asked for nothing in My name; ask and you will receive, so that your joy may be made full". Jesus prayed that his joyful fellowship with Father would spill all over us in John 17:13, "... so that they may have **My** joy made full in themselves"

In these very last days, a deeper understanding of Father's heart is emerging in the church worldwide, as Father is so personally revealing himself. And this greater revelation is causing two very important aspects of our lives to emerge in living color:

- Sonship / Daughterhood
- Kingdom Family

The kingdom of God is organized on different governing principles than the kingdoms of this earth. God could choose any form of government for his country (Heb 11:6) but he simply chose "family". That is, as God himself enjoys constant, eternally rich and joyful fellowship in the Trinity, he extends that joyful fellowship to children won by the blood of Jesus (1 John 1:3, *"what we have seen and heard we proclaim to you also, so that you too may have fellowship with us; and indeed our fellowship is with the Father, and with His Son Jesus Christ"*). Father's overflowing love and expanding joy are cast over us. To the extent that we are able to humble ourselves as children and receive, it first fills us and then overflows (Matt 18:3 *"unless you are converted and become like children, you will not enter the kingdom of heaven"*). This overflow first flows between his children and then to the people all around us. That is his intention and one of the deep and mysterious goals of Calvary.

Jesus is absolutely King of Kings and Lord of Lords but he comes to us with the heart of our big brother (Heb 2:11 *"for which reason He is not ashamed to call them brethren..."*) and we need him to be that for us. We would be so lost without that. And he does so joyfully because he is so glad for us to enter into his joy, his inheritance, and even to share his Father's personal affection toward him (John 17:26 *"...so that the love with which You loved Me may be in them, and I in them"*).

Entering into sonship and daughterhood is eternally important for its own sake as it is the position we will eternally enjoy. But entering into sonship has the important effect of spilling out all over in works of joyful obedience that manifest life in the world. Creation longs for this. The people of the world deeply long to see the manifestation of the purpose and destiny for which they were created. They see this when sons and daughters are revealed who live in the destiny Abba has secretly woven into their cultures, names, and places of living. When they see this, wow, it is seeing the rays of heaven among them. (Clearly, Jesus modelled this among us!!!)

As we enter into sonship and daughterhood we experience the joy of fellowship that is more than enough for us. We don't need any more than this because in this we become so internally rich that we are fully and deeply satisfied. But regardless, sonship comes with birthrights. Although we ourselves are satisfied with our rich fellowship with Father, the world needs us to walk in all of our birthrights because this is how the beauty of destiny is seen on the earth. The rest of this book is about the birthright of Jesus' church becoming manifest as we learn to be sons and daughters. Walking this way is manifesting the culture of heaven here on earth, something very different than what the people of this age are accustomed to.

The bible has many examples of the idea of birthright or of blessings passed on between generations. The blessings passed on to generations were often prophetic and had to do with destiny. The birthright was something more, something that passed on *authority* and position and it is intended to help everyone with this birthright to fulfil that destiny. (See Jacob in Gen 49:1-27). Often the birthright and its authority was given to the firstborn. In the case of Jesus, Father had caused him to inherit the earth, with full authority, and to inherit every promise made by God to man. All the promises are his, period. It is his birthright as firstborn. We understand Jesus as firstborn in the most important ways possible and all the authority of Father rightly falls to him in the new covenant. Jesus was the "firstborn of all creation" (Col 1:15) – although we understand this is an eternal position as he has always been with Father. Jesus was "firstborn from the dead" in his resurrection (see in Col 1:18 and Rev 1:5). All the rights of heaven and its every promise to those on earth are rightly vested in Jesus for all that he is and all he has done.

Importantly, Jesus is also "firstborn among many brothers" as we see in Rom 8:29. This is important because it shows Father's intention that Jesus be *among us in his full birthright*. It is as if fellows on a ship, who labor together for years, suddenly learn that one of their dear shipmates was the prince of the kingdom. In that sense the "birthright" of Jesus is established first to himself and then to his "co-heirs".

We are Jesus co-heirs:

- Galatians 4:7 "You are no longer a slave, but God's child; and since you are his child, God has made you also an heir"
- Rom 8:17 "...and if children, then heirs—heirs of God and fellow heirs with Christ, provided we suffer with him in order that we may also be glorified with him"
- Titus 3:7 "...so that being justified by his grace we might become heirs according to the hope of eternal life"

- Gal 3:29 "And if you are Christ's, then you are Abraham's offspring, heirs according to promise"
- Eph 1:18 "…having the eyes of your hearts enlightened, that you may know what is the hope to which he has called you, what are the riches of his glorious inheritance in the saints"

It is not that we are taking Jesus' birthright as a powerful possession, as if we are seeking power. No, we are not seeking power, we are seeking to enter into the beauty of the Lord by entering into humble, childlike fellowship. That is our sole aim. But we talk about the birthright of the church as a secondary idea – because talking about these birthrights is necessary. It is the birthright of sons and daughters that brings the blessings that the world and its people need. It is what they are waiting for - but it is the *fellowship with God* that we are seeking. Joyful, fulfilling fellowship is our treasure and sole intention.

As Father, Jesus, and Holy Spirit are revealing us into sonship, we are beginning to see how this changes everything and it is what we are to walk in as sons and daughters. We intend to learn to live in the culture of heaven, in God's country and his city – and to learn that country's language.

- Heb 11:16 "But as it is, they desire a better country, that is, a heavenly one. Therefore God is not ashamed to be called their God, for he has prepared for them a city."

- Heb 11:8-10 "By faith Abraham, when he was called, obeyed by going out to a place which he was to receive for an inheritance; and he went out, not knowing where he was going. By faith he lived as an alien in the land of promise, as in a foreign land, dwelling in tents with Isaac and Jacob, fellow heirs of the same promise; for he was looking for the city which has foundations, whose architect and builder is God"

So in the words that follow I want to describe what being sons and daughters means to Jesus' church, his bride, and to the world.

Chapter 2

The Culture of Heaven

The country of heaven is a kingdom whose king is Jesus, but its government is that of "family". God could have chosen any form of government, any pattern of relating, any set of rules and order – but he chose "family" and "relationship" by which all is governed and ordered. Why? Because it most closely reflects his values and the nature of his heart. God himself lives in intense and constant fellowship in the Trinity.

The kingdom of God is family. In its current manifestation we could call it, "a family of families" because there are so many expressions of this family.

One clear theme and message in scripture is that there is only one God, in perfect unity. However, this unity exists in the beautiful, perfect fellowship of Father, Son, and Holy Spirit. There is no jealousy among them, no competition. They all share the same intense joy and love, the same beautiful brilliant mind and heart. They are each God and live in perfect completion but that completion is in part because they are three persons in joyful fellowship. They want to share that intense and joyful fellowship with us. Their intention is for us to know how to enter into that fellowship both as individual people he has made and together in a body he has made (1 John 1:3 says, "so that you too may have fellowship with us; and indeed our fellowship is with the Father, and with His Son Jesus Christ. These things we write, so that our joy may be made complete."). This joyful fellowship is meant to fill creation with his glory.

- Hab 2:14 "For the earth will be filled with the knowledge of the glory of the LORD, as the waters cover the sea".
- Eph 1:22,23 "... and gave Him as head over all things to the church, which is His body, *the fullness of Him who fills all in all*".
- Isa 11:9 "...for the earth will be full of the knowledge of the Lord as the waters cover the sea".

One day I was at church and I was feeling like crap, really. And I apologized to Jesus because I did not feel *any* motivation to worship. I knew he deserves worship and he has been really good to me. But I was honest with him. He said that he understood and that he loves to worship. That did not make sense to me because how can he worship since he himself is God and entirely one with Father and Holy Spirit. I felt "internal theological conflict". Then he said, "come and see" and immediately I was in a vision where I saw Jesus in the Trinity. Jesus kept telling the truth to Father about his beauty, love, perfection and Father kept telling Jesus how much he loved him and how perfectly he has always obeyed him. They also were telling Holy Spirit beautiful things together. The love, joy, and pure and holy truth they were sharing was hot like the sun and hard to stay close to. Was it "worship", was it love, was it intense fellowship, was it a bath of pure joy between them? It was more than I could manage. I felt Jesus reach his hand out from behind himself, just outside this intense loving circle, to take my hand. He wanted me to know that he could be mindful of me even in this place of intense fellowship. He wanted me to understand something of God himself as well and something of the real worship we will experience in eternity. That is, worship is not some kind of religious flattery, it is a whole heart speaking truth to another whole and fully present heart - and in the case of God, that truth just happens to be intensely marvelous.

We have just begun to know God, especially Father. We have eternity to enjoy the process. Think of this a moment: there are certain angels near God, they never cease in worship. But they do not do it because it's their job, its simply because they are very close to a stream of continually unfolding beauty. As intelligent, curious beings, they are in a continual state of marvel and wonder. I think that in human language, when they continually say "glory!" it is very much like they are saying "WOW!"

Learning to Know God as Father:

In the mid-1980's we were learning about the Father Heart of God. The things we learned dramatically changed our lives and many of the people around us as we began to both discover the character of God as Father and to learn paths to healing. In these days the Lord has been showing a far deeper and richer understanding of what his Father heart means as he is teaching us to know *sonship* and *kingdom family*.

The path of our growth and understanding began with seeing with new eyes Jesus' teaching and revelation of his Father in the gospels. Jesus both taught and modelled the love of Father. We began to understand what Jesus said about Father's character when he said, "the Father himself loves you" (John 16:27). This was a radical shift for our understanding because the structure of our thinking was built so much out of religion and he wanted us to learn to live in genuine relationship with he and Father. That is to say, the reality of Father and our connection to him has completely eclipsed the ideas we had of him, many of which were just religion. We began to see even more of Father's character as we understood that Jesus was perfectly modelling his Father ("he who has seen me has seen the Father" John 14:9).

At the same time, we began to understand the gap between *our experience* of Father's love from that of *our understanding* of it. That is, we could agree with it theologically but we really needed to be baptized in it (Rom 5:5 "...because the love of God has been poured out within our hearts through the Holy Spirit who was given to us"). The intention of Father was not that we would merely *change our thinking* but that we would *encounter him in his true nature*. In this our thinking would naturally change. This was never meant to be an exercise of greater understanding or of correcting our theological position but a profound revelation of his genuine nature, genuine presence, and a life-changing encounter.

This encounter is like the act of a toddler walking. That is, to move forward we must initiate a fall, *leaning toward the loving face we see*, while lifting one of our feet and placing it just ahead of our position to catch ourselves, then falling forward again and moving our other foot ahead. We alternate feet and ever so slightly fall forward with each step, left, right, left, right. This is a good analogy of how we learn to know Father. The encounter or revelation is initiated by seeing a glimpse of Father ahead of us, his beaming face, his open arms, and we feel a surge of joy. Then we fall forward by stepping out in humility as a child to receive. One step is healing, one step is revelation, in continual sequence.

In our need and pain we are urgent to receive healing and the healing comes from finding that he was with us in our pain, and we see who he was as he stood alongside us. As we see great vistas into his heart, this revelation by its nature touches on our pain and heals it. Love that is real, powerful, and tangible always heals. It "sets the bones" of our experience and comforts us.

This healing process will continue our whole lives until he wipes away every tear from our eyes in his presence (Rev 7:17 and 21:4).

Jesus revealed Father to us in all that he did. He revealed God to as us Father because that is his genuine nature in all his goodness. The heart of his Father is something that he sincerely and earnestly wants us to know. Core to Jesus' mission, the most important undertaking of history, was to reveal Father to us because he really wants us to know his Father.

> Matt 11:27 "All things have been handed over to Me by My Father; and no one knows the Son except the Father; nor does anyone know the Father except the Son, and anyone to whom the Son wills to reveal Him" (see also Luke 10:22).

In light of the fact that this is so important to Jesus, we should take this as very important ourselves. We set ourselves firmly on this goal, to know Father as Jesus intended.

David A. Melander

The Culture of Heaven:

As we refer to the "culture of heaven" we are acknowledging the basic concept that "culture" (by definition) is a shared way of seeing the world, ourselves, its people, and how all of it is structured and understood. "Culture" is also used to describe the way the customs and activities of people manifest the intangibles of shared understandings. In this definition we understand that the "culture of heaven" is the shared knowledge (the understanding and perspective of Father) and the shared language of heaven (the language of love).

In the case of heaven, shared knowledge is truth, not "perspective". The shared knowledge of heaven is truth because it is both (a) *a living knowledge of a person* from whom all "truth" emanates (see John 14:6 "I am...the truth...") and (b) it is an understanding or worldview that emanates from the person *from whom all things exist*. So our "understanding" of the world, ourselves, its people, and the interrelationship of all things comes in a simple act of "seeing as God sees". In this sense it is not an "alternate perspective" to the perspectives of others (as in, "that's *your* truth") but it is holding on a heart-level things that are in fact fundamentally true because these things flow from the one who understands the world in its most fundamental way. That is, he is the one who knows the secrets of the quanta, the one who creates and maintains the molecular "strong force" (see Col 1:17, Heb 1:3), the one who truly knows the hearts of all men (see John 2:24) and their truest identity and destiny. That knowledge in all respects supersedes all the mental constructs of men called "truth".

In living from the culture of heaven we don't need to argue with people about matters of "perspective" ("small 't' truth"). When we do that we reduce our position from heaven to earth, we lower ourselves to a conversation solely on an earthly level. All the arguments of the world are like children playing in the sandbox and arguing about what Spiderman's shoes are made of. They can argue heatedly with great conviction all the while Spiderman is in fact a fictional character, they are talking in circles of elements of fiction, however true to them it becomes. While the argument seems "real to them" the only things truly present and real are they themselves, the sand in the box, and the one truly present but invisible among them. In that sense, when we walk in heaven's culture we recognize the reality of Jesus' presence in every situation and how this completely supersedes all other "perspectives" that are merely human constructs, a reality that supersedes truths of a small letter "t".

We learned this, and it may be a helpful perspective:

- Jesus is the TRUTH (that is, he fully embodies all truth because he is the source of creation and order)

- The bible is the "truth" about the "TRUTH"
- Our doctrines, our perspectives and opinions, may be "truths about the truth about the TRUTH"

All the ideas in the world may be "true" in the sense that they may be accurate or that they may accurately reflect a person's life experience or perspective. And as human beings we can honor people and ideas that come from their perspective. We do that because giving honor to someone is a path toward having our eyes open to see the destiny of God for them, something that he is longing for in them. However, human ideas are sometimes little more than instincts learned by culture, teaching, and experience, made mostly of electro-chemical impulses in the brain. Still we honor people while knowing the TRUTH exists in all his glory, whether people know it or not.

The shared knowledge in heaven's culture supersedes all of human experience. It is first the knowledge *of the person of God in our fellowship with him* and second it is sharing with him all the things he knows about each situation, everywhere we go, because we are able to share the mind of Christ (1 Cor 2:16 "but you have the mind of Christ", Phil 2:5-8 "have this mind in you which was also in Christ Jesus...").

There are two ways in which we are told we have (*or are urged to have*) the "mind of Christ". 1 Cor 2:16 describes a gift that the Holy Spirit gives us to enable us to understand the things of God. Phil 2:5-8 describes coming to have the *mind of Christ* in the *attitude* of Christ. You might call this second "mind of Christ" as "having his heart". Either way, the thoughts and attitude of Christ are intended to be available to us. We actually need it and there are many promises in scripture that describe this wonderful gift. Here are just a few examples:

1. In John 16:12,13 Jesus said "I have many more things to say to you, but you cannot bear them now. But when He, the Spirit of truth, comes, He will guide you into all the truth; for He will not speak on His own initiative, but whatever He hears, He will speak; and He will disclose to you what is to come. He will glorify Me, for He will take of Mine and will disclose it to you. All things that the Father has are Mine; therefore I said that He takes of Mine and will disclose it to you."

So Jesus wants us to learn things from the Holy Spirit as he searches the mind and heart of Jesus and Father and then reveals them to us.

2. Jesus also told us that Holy Spirit would teach us what we need to know. John 14:26: "But the Helper, the Holy Spirit, whom the Father will send in My name, He will teach you all things, and bring to your remembrance all that I said to you."

3. We know that the Holy Spirit also gives people gifts of prophecy to understand what he wants us to know, discernment of spirits to understand and see the true nature of things, words of knowledge and words of wisdom to understand things we could not understand or know on our own.

These are all important examples of promises to us that we should take very literally and believe them. They are means that we come to know the mind of Christ and Father.

One time I visited a class that a friend of mine was teaching. I did not feel connected to anyone and was feeling lonely. I was feeling a little disconnected to God also. But I asked Father if he wanted me to know something. Then I saw a vision of the person next to me, a vision of hands clasped like cabbage leaves around a very little baby. I could see the baby and suddenly knew that this person's mother had tried to abort her. I could discern some serious rejection vibes on her also. But instead of saying anything to her I asked God for his heart. He told me that she would feel more rejected if I said something to her so he told me not to single her out, just share the vision with the class. That gentle way would not make the rejection go deeper. I shared the vision and she immediately shouted, "that's me, my mother tried to abort me!" And then we sweetly prayed for her to receive healing. She received a revelation from Father how he had protected her and how he so deeply wants her. I am glad that I received both the information from God and shared the heart of God so that she could be deeply healed. If I had only the information, she may have felt more rejection and not the healing the Lord has for her.

Sweetly, Jesus said, "my sheep hear My voice, and I know them, and they follow Me; and I give eternal life to them, and they will never perish; and no one will snatch them out of My hand" (John 10:27,28). So we can really rely on this. We as sheep are intended to hear his voice and he will share with us his mind on any issue. We do need, however, to humble ourselves as children.

But here is the rub, sometimes there are things that make it hard to know the mind of God, even if the Holy Spirit wants us to understand it. There are of course many things like demonic interference (think Daniel and the Prince of Persia...Dan 10:13). But mostly I think the obstacles are issues of the heart. I think that Father does not want so much for us to get *information* as he does *transformation*. It is kind of like the tree of knowledge vs the tree of life. Do we want power through knowledge? He knows it would hurt us to have access to too much knowledge because knowledge can puff us up or make us proud. But if we are willing to "know first" or "know best" all that is on his heart, that keeps us from pride because it draws us close to him and makes us like him (because we begin to see him).

So, for me, when I want to understand Father's mind on an issue, I try and make myself soft and vulnerable to him and the things stirring in him. Do that first because it makes our heart like that of Father and Jesus. Then we have the capacity to receive more "revelation" of things that won't make us proud.

Just to sum this up, the shared knowledge of the country of heaven is sharing the mind of God and living in the culture of heaven means sharing Father's brilliant perspective by the simple act of maintaining connection with him. That is the "shared knowledge" of heaven, the base of heaven's culture.

But culture also means having a shared language. In heaven that language is the language of love. The grammar and vocabulary in the home of God, in the bosom of the Father, is love. Little pieces ("clues") of that language are reflected in all 15,000 languages on earth. As we speak below of *kingdom family* and *sonship* and *daughterhood*, we describe the vocabulary of heaven's language.

One day I was driving on Interstate 94 through Minneapolis and I was suddenly caught up into heaven. Sounds dangerous. Worse, I was in the infamous Lowry Hill Tunnel. Really, I have no idea how you can have a vision like that in a tunnel. I think angels may know how to drive. But in heaven I met a man. He was sharing with me simple truths in incredibly articulate language. I struggled so hard to understand him and I felt incredibly dull. I asked him to speak slowly or to repeat several times. I knew that I really should understand what he was speaking because it was actually simple, but it was so different in construct and vocabulary and patterned so differently than my own way of speaking/thinking. I did my best to capture what he was saying because I knew he was speaking something on behalf of the will of heaven.

When I came out of the vision Father asked me a question. He asked me what I noticed about the man. I could not think of anything, so he patiently asked me again. I tried to remember the man's face but all I could think of was being in awe of his articulate speech and impressive understanding. In the next moment I could slowly see and remember something of the man and was very surprised that he had had Down's Syndrome while he was on earth. And Father asked me again a simple question, "what language was he speaking?", and I was trying hard to remember but I could not recall any of his words. I thought how I had tried to keep up with him. Then it struck me he was not using words but speaking in a very fundamental way from the movements of his heart. I understood in that moment that the language of heaven is love. Then Father told me that the most eloquent people in heaven learned the language of love in sacrificial living in their earthly life. That "sacrificial living" was not religious at all, but joyful, flowing from a heart that genuinely wants to exchange temporal things for eternal joy and beauty.

David A. Melander

Sonship and Kingdom Family:

In these very last days, a deeper understanding of Father's heart is emerging in the church worldwide, as Father is so personally revealing himself in sonship/daughterhood and Kingdom Family.

The sections that follow dive deeply into what it means to really have a revelation of being a son or daughter and of living in a family together as real kin. Learning the culture of heaven is a big adjustment because we are so familiar with our own ethnic culture and family culture (and even "church culture!") and we live in these familiar things without thinking. We are just beginning to understand how true it is that Father's thoughts are much higher than ours.

As we experience our secure place as sons and daughters in the house of Father, paid for eternally by Jesus, as we develop this secure connection with Father and lose the need to compete, we see others in their brilliant destiny, we see abundance instead of lack and have a new and generous nature. It becomes our native language.

The entire creation now longs for the revelation of the sons of God. Again, Rom 8:19 told us that creation is anxiously longing for the revealing of the sons of God, to see the glorious freedom of the sons of God so that creation is free from death, futility, and corruption. It is like creation feels the pains of childbirth.

As we begin to live in sonship and freedom, the sons of God become manifest or revealed. The result is the glory of the Lord begins to fill his creation.

Chapter 3

Kingdom Family

The governance of the country of heaven is managed in family and relationship. This is what most pleases Father because it comes from his heart. If you wonder if that could be true, think of how Jesus modeled it. Read the story of the "prodigal son" in Luke, how his father longed for him, watched for him, waited for him, and *ran* to him. Think of how Father kissed his stinky son (he had been some years with the pigs...) before he even cleaned him up. That says a lot.

As we said before, living in the culture of heaven means sharing Father's brilliant perspective by the simple act of maintaining connection with him. This is the "shared knowledge" of heaven, the base of heaven's culture. But culture also means having a shared language. In heaven that language is the language of love. The most eloquent people in heaven learned the language of love in sacrificial living in their earthly life. They live that way because they come to prefer Father's wisdom, perspective, and loving attitude over their own natural way of thinking. They want Father's ideas because they are truly beautiful (Ps 27:4). That is basic and essential to being a person "after God's own heart."

Kingdom family:

I know I am repeating, but in these very last days, a deeper understanding of Father's heart is emerging in the church worldwide, as Father is so personally revealing himself. And as we said, this greater revelation is causing two very important aspects of our lives to emerge:

- Sonship / Daughterhood
- Kingdom Family

What do we mean by "Kingdom Family?" Kingdom Family is the simple concept of learning to live together while we grow to understand what it means to be a son or a daughter.

Here are some principles that guide us:

A. We are real family. This is because each of us shares a living connection with our Father, we are truly kin and we share so much together:
   1. We will be family in heaven forever in intense fellowship where we see the real beauty in

each other, even though that is not yet fully visible here.
2. We share the same promises. We are those who inherit the promises, but we can only do this as we share this mission or adventure together. It is too hard alone because we have limitations in our faith and strength.
3. We share the same mission in the world to share Jesus and continue his mission. "So Jesus said to them again, 'Peace be with you; as the Father has sent Me, I also send you.'" John 20:21.
4. We have access to Papa together – individually but even more when we do this together.

B. We learn to see each other through our Father's eyes. We are happy to do so. As we are in a celebration of every individual:
1. Celebrate what people are, not focusing in on what they are "*not yet*".
2. We believe in each person's destiny in Father and we are excited for it.
3. We see how they are made in the image of God.
4. We open our spiritual eyes to recognize the gifts Father has given each one and we make space for their gifts. We encourage them as they attempt to take some steps.
5. We are excited to see the presence of Holy Spirit in them.

6. We see that each one, as followers of Jesus and in knowing each person of the Trinity, is now in a position to start to fulfill the beautiful destiny that Father has held in his heart for their clans and families over generations.

C. We truly value each other and show this by honoring each other.

D. We together treasure and earnestly value the presence of the Lord in us, even an intense presence that often manifests in glory, or power, or awe. Why? Even in the center of intense manifestations of Jesus presence, there is the beauty of his character. Although Jesus is intensely powerful, his heart of humility, meekness, gentleness, and transparency is right there because of his sincere desire to be known. The fragrance of his presence is sweet, even while intense.

E. Miracles are natural in the family, this is a supernatural family because our Papa is present, with Jesus and Holy Spirit.

F. Glory and beauty is the real state of the family of families we call church.

G. Real community emerges because we no longer compete with each other in our celebration of each other.

H. We experience genuine belonging as we go beyond surface level in our relationships. We have a heart connection in a family because we have individually become securely attached sons and daughters with our Father.

I. Generosity is a common trait of the culture of heaven. Valuing people above material or possessions shows that our hearts are "taken" with heaven and this expression naturally flows from our secure connection with Father.

Living these principles out are an expression of the language of heaven, but they are also our birthrights as sons and daughters.

We speak the language of heaven, the language of love, in actions and words - its structural grammar being attitudes and its vocabulary being action and words. For the sake of clarity, I do mean that this is *an actual language* in heaven that takes the form of communication in that realm.

I acknowledge that the vocabulary of the language of heaven is not yet clearly being spoken commonly in the body of Christ. As it is emerging in his people, it comes out as baby talk - babbling - and not in full sentences. The language of honor, for example, has been learned by some and we hear it when we are with them. I saw and experienced so much of this when I was with some friends in Malaysia in March of 2019 at a "Kingdom Family Gathering". Sonship, kingdom family, honor, and generosity were in the air everywhere.

The language begins to mature in us from this specific foundation, that we learn our secure place as sons and daughters in the house of Father, paid for eternally by Jesus. As we develop this secure connection with Father we lose the need to compete, we see others in their brilliant destiny, we see abundance instead of lack and have a new and generous nature. It becomes our native language.

As we try and "tune-in" to heaven's language, in order to learn its vocabulary, we must learn by listening, as we would learn any language. In this case we listen to Holy Spirit as our personal language instructor. To do this, we must learn to connect with him often during the day. Frequently we hear the voice of the Holy Spirit inside that asks on behalf of Father whether we are acting as children, not as orphans or slaves, and he asks us if we are calling those around us to sonship. This voice is a strong magnet that pulls us firmly toward true north, toward truth as Father sees. In that way we are beginning to be a living example of the culture of heaven even while we are here on earth.

For example, I was asked to teach for 14 hours at a local ministry on using prophetic gifts in evangelism.

I had agreed to teach without thinking much about the topic. But then I started thinking, "what do I know about this?" I asked my wife, Adri, if I should cancel. She laughed and said, "you do prophetic evangelism all the time". I said, "I do???" and she reminded me of many of my life experiences where I have done that. I thought to myself, "oh, I guess that's what they mean, I just thought of those stories of just being with Jesus…" Similarly, I was scheduled to teach for a week at another ministry on using prophetic gifts. I really was serious about preparing, but as I thought over and over about what to teach, nothing was really coming to me. I asked the Lord with some intensity to help me, to give me some direction or guidance on what to teach. He so confidently and gently said that I was "not there to teach". I said, "I think I *am* there to teach, they are expecting me to teach." But Jesus told me, "I want you there not to teach but to model, to model what it looks like when someone stays connected to me."

The entire, mature, eloquent language of love, all of its grammar and vocabulary, is built on the simple foundation of each person becoming a true son or daughter. The full reward of the suffering of the Lamb of God is fulfilled when his family are bathed in fellowship together, filled with love, and this love starts to spill out all over. It is Father that awakens this language in us as we begin to experience:

- A secure attachment to Father, and of course, with Jesus and Holy Spirit at the same time. We grow in this secure attachment simply by responding bravely to his invitations to fellowship moment by moment.
- The secure knowledge we have a place in his family and we no longer compete. Rather we begin to imitate our Father, to see as he sees, to be generous like he is.

Living in Kingdom Family values is a deep expression of being a daughter or son. It will become natural to us as we live it. And as we begin to live in sonship and freedom, the sons of God become manifest or revealed. The result is the glory of the Lord begins to fill his creation.

Chapter 4

Father's Movement

Jesus is bringing us into his very own relationship with Father (John 17:26) so that we can complete His mission to close out the age (John 20:21). He wants sons and daughters to live in simple faith and walk with him.

Here I want to share some thoughts about why Father is being so personally revealed to us now, why this is important now at this point in history.

It should be fairly obvious to all of us that this is the last throes of the "present evil age": Matt 24:3 – 31; Luke 21:10 – 19; Mark 13:3 – 13:

1. Famine
2. Earthquake
3. War, genocide ("rumors of war")
4. Epidemics

Jesus described the very last of days as characterized by the things listed above. And you probably know that throughout history there have always been wars, famines, earthquakes and so on. These were in part manifested in the time immediately after Jesus death and resurrection in the difficult times that came upon Jerusalem up to its destruction in 70 AD.

Yet, in our lifetimes we are seeing a more profound fulfillment of Jesus' words. There has been a very profound threshold crossed - the nature of events in famine, earthquake, war and genocide, and in epidemics has become quantitatively different. Starting around 1948 or so, around the time of another important prophetic event, the establishment of Israel as a nation, the effects of these things, even the nature of these things, crossed important and quantitative lines.

Famine, for example, has always been with mankind we could say. But today there are approximately four times as many people in serious lack of food *as there were alive* at the time Jesus spoke these words. If you look at the graph of world population over time and a graph of persons in serious malnutrition you will find somewhere around 1948 there were as many people starving in the modern world as *there were people alive* at the time Jesus told us about it. That is a clear threshold.

Similarly, if we look at earthquakes, most of the very serious earthquakes, when measured by death and casualty, occurred since 1900. The most serious occurred in my own lifetime. This is simply because since around 1948 (give or take...) the move toward urbanization (formation of large cities) started to accelerate. If you just consider the Tangshan earthquake in the 1980's, where 800,000+ people died, you will see a stark picture. Clearly we have crossed a threshold.

War? Same. Consider in the last century, my father Don's lifetime, by some estimates, approximately as many people died in wars and rumors of war (I call "rumors of war" genocides and hidden wars) as were alive at the time Jesus said this. Threshold, yes.

Epidemics, the same can be said in many ways. AIDS, SARS, the 1918 Flu,...

We could actually be frightened by these things except that our dear Father is sending us such great comfort!!!

I want you to consider the flip side of all this trouble. This is also the time of greatest revival (also in Matt 24) the world has ever known, with millions coming to Christ. Consider these:

1. Several hundred million persons have come to Christ in my father's lifetime. Consider just the revival in China in the last 100 years where perhaps 100 million persons have come to know the dear Lord Jesus.
2. Places where these was no church or witness now have a church. I think of a friend who went to an "unreached" people group and when he

got there, he found intense revival already in full bloom. He married one of the evangelists there! Missions experts say that we are close to having a bible in every language and a church among most people groups. That is encouraging.
3. A great time of harvest among Muslim people groups is imminently upon us, as are times of harvest among Hindu people groups, and in Japan.

So this is both a time of difficulty and a time of glory for the church (revival, "presence" that we have not known, miracles, and intense fellowship with Father).

Mike Bickle of The International House of Prayer (IHOP) speaks about days of tribulation and of victory co-existing. The IHOP statement says, "We will go through it ("tribulation") in great victory and power"[1].

Bill Johnson said:

> We live at a time when it seems that the evil of this world is becoming more pronounced, while the glory of God in the Church is also being put on display in more glorious and obvious manners... For me this word helps settle the tension

---

[1] See https://ihop-kc.livejournal.com/901.html for IHOP's detailed position statement.

we face anytime we discuss the subject of the last days – darkness and light both increasing[2].

God's glory and presence are "native" to the church and will be restored like a beacon of light during difficult days. (More about that in a chapter that follows).

The church worldwide has experienced much renewal in the last 100 years but we could not contain everything Father intended. We have been thrilled by Holy Spirit's presence and in this day our Father intends his people to fully receive the baptism of love spoken of in Rom 5:5, because we are now coming to *know* and to *believe* the love the God has for us (1 John 4:16) in a new and deeper way, beyond our experience and imagination.

In the modern era the Lord has been restoring to His church to a relationship with him. Starting in the 1730's in the Pietist movements and Wesleyanism, through the Great Awakening in the US and elsewhere, the Lord was reintroducing a basic concept of having a personal relationship with Jesus Christ. This movement affected people worldwide with the message of knowing Christ personally and it continues to this day. This is the message of salvation.

- What keeps people from coming into this relationship is human pride and that a veil covers our eyes by the prince of the power of the air.

---

[2] Bill Johnson from the Introduction, Heavy Rain - How To Flood Your World with Gods Transforming Power
Kris Vallotton - Baker Publishing Group - 2016

During the Pentecostal and Charismatic movements of the 20th century the Lord was reintroducing the importance of a personal relationship with the Holy Spirit. Denominational churches worldwide experienced a new life and wind of the Spirit. This continues to be the fastest growing Christian movement in the world.

- What keeps people from experiencing a relationship with the Holy Spirit is related in part to veils of religious ideas and religious forces that try and keep people from experiencing the freedom and joy of having him in our lives.

Now the Lord is moving in His church across the world reintroducing himself as Father, wooing his church to personal relationship with Abba.

- The Father Himself loves his children and wants us each to know that in a way that *wins our hearts*, such that we are drawn joyfully into seeking him and knowing him.
- What keeps us from knowing him in this way are the veils of our life experiences and the lies of our cultures.

This movement is both a healing movement and a revival.

- We understand it as a healing movement because one of the ways that Father shows himself to us is by revealing his nature in contrast to our life experience - and that transforms our inward thinking.
- That is, for example, for those who have wounds from "absent" fathers, he reveals himself as the Father who loves to be continually present with his whole-hearted and joyful self.
- We also understand this as a healing movement because we will become family, holding each other through the healing.
- Worldwide fatherless generations wherever they are on this small world, are being won to his heart.
- These doors of love are a supernatural revelation of Father's heart that will sweep into the church.
- That will be another wave of revival with manifestations of healing and the supernatural but of something much deeper, a manifestation of God's heart being born in us corporately and individually.

There are several characteristics of the results of this baptism of love:

1. The deep riches of Father's love are a resource that helps us have freedom from the bondage to materialism. Our hearts become like Father

as we learn to value people more than material, just as Father values them. They are eternal.

2. As people are deeply baptized in the Love of Father (see Rom 5:5) they are taken up with a spirit of generosity. We see people become full and rich as Father is full and rich and in this they become like their Father.

   a) See Matt 5:45 – 48 "...so that you may be sons of your Father who is in heaven; for He causes His sun to rise on the evil and the good, and sends rain on the righteous and the unrighteous. For if you love those who love you, what reward do you have? Do not even the tax collectors do the same? If you greet only your brothers, what more are you doing than others? Do not even the Gentiles do the same? Therefore you are to be perfect, as your heavenly Father is perfect". (see also Luke 6:35 – 36)
   b) This is what happened in Acts 2:44 ff: "And all those who had believed were together and had all things in common; and they began selling their property and possessions and were sharing them with all, as anyone might have need. Day by day continuing with one mind in the temple, and breaking bread from house to house, they

were taking their meals together with gladness and sincerity of heart, praising God and having favor with all the people. And the Lord was adding to their number day by day those who were being saved". I believe this is one aspect of the unfinished work that was intended in the heart of God to come from the Holy Spirit revivals of the 1980's.

3. People touched deeply in this baptism of the Father's love know his strength, confidence, and authority. They are able to walk in dark places without fear just as Jesus walked, *seeing the dark while keeping their eyes on Father as Jesus did*. They have no fear of people who are different or of people who are captured in strange or occult groups because they see Abba's dream and vision of what they are meant to become.

4. The healing that Father's love has brought to their heart flows out of them and makes them willing to embrace other's in their pain without judgment, in patience, in confidence and maturity, not being overwhelmed but trusting in Father's bigness.

5. The people who are baptized in Father's heart have a deep and very natural love toward the seed of Abraham. They do not need to adopt

any outward signs of affinity to Jewish things, like wearing prayer shawls or reciting Jewish prayers, but from the heart they love the seed in the heart of every Jewish man or woman. A natural and generous love flows out of them.

6. The people deeply baptized in Father's heart love all that he loves. For example, they see the beautiful destiny for the sons of Ishmael and love him for what he is about to become.

7. New joy will characterize the church as we each learn from Father our own joyful, personal identity, the name that he speaks over us and from our sense of deep belongingness with the Father. John 15:11, "These things I have spoken to you so that My joy may be in you, and that your joy may be made full."

There are specific outcomes in the church which we will soon see in increasing measure among us:

1. He makes his home in us. John 14:23. His dwelling in us will make his character revealed to the world and to all of his dear children.

2. The process of his self-revelation to the church begins to "wipe away every tear", the beginning of the fulfillment of Rev 7:17 and Rev 21:4.

In partnership with people in healing prayer, brave and deep confession, forgiveness, intercession – giving each other life as we receive it for each other directly from Father.

3. He carries them in his arms through hard times, strength for things his people will face in the days to come, lending his children his great strength to stand. We will know Father with us as Jesus knew Father with him in his passion (see John 16:32, "Behold, an hour is coming, and has already come, for you to be scattered, each to his own home, and to leave Me alone; and yet I am not alone, because the Father is with Me").

4. Jesus warned us that in these days the love of many will grow cold (Matt 24:12). The forces behind the "falling away" are already loosed on the earth (1 Tim 4:1). Father is sending us his heart so that our love will not grow cold. See 1 John 2:15, "Do not love the world nor the things in the world. If anyone loves the world, the love of the Father is not in him" (conversely, when the love of Father *is* in him, the love of the world begins to fall away).

5. Father is sending us his heart as part of the spirit of Elijah to help turn the hearts of fathers toward children and children toward fathers. As

Father's heart breaks into our woundedness with his sweetness, we are able to love those who've wounded us. Jesus began this work (Luke 1:17) and Father is finishing it with him.

This movement is not about preaching but about revelation. It is not about "right thinking" but an inner revelation and a *saturating baptism*. This revelation is where Father reveals himself for who he truly is, how he truly *wants* to relate with us, his desire for connection.

Preaching must occur but it cannot alone bring revelation.

I want to give you an example of the gap between understanding and knowing. For example, when we lived in Indonesia, sometimes the subject of conversation at lunch would casually include things that happened to people, their stories and experiences. On some occassions these stories included someone present at lunch with us being someone who had been raised from the dead. This was shocking to me as an American. But in the context of conversation it was almost casual, normal, and they seemed fully accustomed to it. This really confused me. I never saw that in America. When I asked the Lord to explain this to me he simply let me know that my friends there really believed in Jesus own resurrection and in his tangible presence among them. As a result it was entirely natural that things like this would happen around him, that is, around the present Jesus. In a moment

I understood the difference between assent to a concept and knowing its reality. That is, we all believe in Jesus' resurrection, but some of us *really* believe in it. In the same way, we all accept that Father so loved the world, but it is treated in our deep internal thinking as "code" for something else. Something like, "well of course if God was about being 'good' he would be loving". But those inner spaces in our hearts may not have grasped the personal passion he feels and our inner thoughts may reduce the love of Father in our inner thinking to something more like simple "condescension" in place of a personal, passionate, intentional feeling from Father's heart. The understanding of the love of Father must move from being a religious idea we share into a deep inner revelation that changes us from the ground up. Preaching alone cannot do that. It requires a revelation and a saturating baptism.

The baptism we are talking about is the Rom 5 baptism, the love of Father God being shed abroad in our hearts by Holy Spirit. It is meant to be a saturating baptism that by its extent touches us profoundly, deeply through all our parts and secret chambers of the heart. He is intending to be known for who he really is and as we see it, we change.

In 1 John it says that we have come to *know* and have *believed* the love Father has for us. I think that we start with believing but we end in "knowing":

- That is a knowing of our whole self, not a knowing of the mind.
- It is a knowing that reaches to the secret inner places of our hearts and souls where our deepest doubts and fears control us.
- That is on this deep, inner level that the baptism (the *saturating* baptism) is meant to reach.
- We are to literally be *embraced* by love on that level, such that the smallest, weakest, most voiceless parts of ourselves find a safe and permanent home of light where they have immediate access to Father's heart.

This is core to the mission of Calvary. Jesus came to seek and save the lost, not to "save" them just from destruction, but to *bring them to the Father*. This is important. It is at the heart of Jesus' sacrifice and must be taken seriously. Our experience of fellowship with God as sons and daughters is indeed critically integrated in the Lamb receiving the full reward of his suffering. It has become our birthright. Being family and living as children is at the core of heaven's culture.

Chapter 5

The Destiny of Peoples

People do not exist randomly across the face of this planet, as if the people of the world exist solely by chance in random or meaningless lives. Culture, names, traditions, and places show the hand of artistry, the beautiful hand of God:

Sons and daughters who come into the destiny designed by their Father manifest beauty where they are and their glory shows Father's glory.

I was someone's best man at his wedding and it meant, among many things, standing in a long line and shaking hands with a couple hundred strangers. Since I am a friendly person this was kind of fun for me. To one person in the line I said something funny, it was spontaneous and I wonder what I might have said if I had any planning or forethought. I said, "oh, I see you just came back from Kenya". That was funny because we did not know each other and there was NO way that I could know that. But I knew that because the Holy Spirit had shown me that she had been with some people in Kenya who love and worship Jesus. There was something of their glory still on her. I could see it. That may sound weird but to me it was a tangible reality. It says something of the destiny of people from east Africa. Many people who have spent time there will immediately recognize what I am saying. My experience of seeing the worshiper's beauty on a stranger at a wedding is simple evidence about the glory of people who come into destiny and that how destiny spills over onto others.

Every tribe, language group, clan, and family is not only known to Father, in his heart he holds a dream for them. We can call Father's desires and dreams "destiny". This dream is something that is so perfectly "fit" to them that when someone comes into that dream, amazing beauty immediately begins to bloom in outrageous color. That is because Father really knows people and really loves people.

The bible tells us two important clues to destiny:

- Destiny revealed in the place of our origin
- Destiny revealed in our name

Destiny of peoples as revealed in their situation or place of origin:

David A. Melander

Babel did not end in disaster but because of Father's wonderful wisdom it ends in a great recovery:

- Gen 11:1 – 9 Now the whole earth used the same language and the same words. It came about as they journeyed east, that they found a plain in the land of Shinar and settled there. They said to one another, "Come, let us make bricks and burn them thoroughly." And they used brick for stone, and they used tar for mortar. They said, "Come, let us build for ourselves a city, and a tower whose top will reach into heaven, and let us make for ourselves a name, otherwise we will be scattered abroad over the face of the whole earth." The LORD came down to see the city and the tower which the sons of men had built. The LORD said, "Behold, they are one people, and they all have the same language. And this is what they began to do, and now nothing which they purpose to do will be impossible for them. "Come, let Us go down and there confuse their language, so that they will not understand one another's speech." So the LORD scattered them abroad from there over the face of the whole earth; and they stopped building the city. Therefore, its name was called Babel, because there the LORD confused the language of the whole

earth; and from there the LORD scattered them abroad over the face of the whole earth.
- Acts 17:26 – 28 "and He made from one man every nation of mankind to live on all the face of the earth, having determined their appointed times and the boundaries of their habitation, that they would seek God, if perhaps they might grope for Him and find Him, though He is not far from each one of us; for in Him we live and move and exist, as even some of your own poets have said, 'For we also are His children.'..."

Paul's message in Acts 17 acknowledges that the whole earth is inhabited by mankind, and the peoples are set in each location with some divine intention. It was not random or the whim of people as to where and when they would settle. There was divine intention for eternally, brilliant reasons that are tied to the destiny of those people before the throne (see Rev 7:9, below).

Paul's message also makes clear that the times of habitation and locations of habitation are intended for a divine and good purpose, that we would be caused or provoked to "grope for him" and seek him even though he is actually very close to each of us.

Clearly, the intention of Father God *is that we find Him* in the place and time he has placed our people.

Good news:

We see that God's intention is to bring people back together at the end of all things:

- Rev 7:9: "After these things I looked, and behold, a great multitude which no one could count, from every nation and all tribes and peoples and tongues, standing before the throne and before the Lamb, clothed in white robes, and palm branches were in their hands"

We see that this was his intention, revealed throughout scripture (examples):

- Gen 49:10: "The scepter shall not depart from Judah, nor the ruler's staff from between his feet, until Shiloh comes, and to him *shall be the obedience of the peoples*" (speaking of Jesus the Messiah)
- Psa 2:8 "Ask of Me, and I will surely give the nations as Your inheritance, And the very ends of the earth as Your possession" (God speaking, addressing Messiah, his begotten son)
- Psa 22:27 "All the ends of the earth will remember and turn to the LORD, and all the families of the nations will worship before You"
- Isa 49:6 He says, "It is too small a thing that You should be My Servant to raise up the tribes

of Jacob and to restore the preserved ones of Israel; I will also make You a light of the nations so that My salvation may reach to the end of the earth" (speaking of Jesus the Messiah)

We understand that at Babel the evil one wanted to extend his hold on mankind by extending his original lie, "they shall be like God." His intention was to use mankind to gain access to heaven for his own purposes, for power and for a false and tainted glory. The result for mankind would have been a deepening of mankind's slavery to evil.

In God's intentional mercy, he caused a scattering of mankind in order to preserve in each of the clan's of mankind some part of His original "investment" of his image. These, the pieces forming the whole, are brought together at the Throne. A recovery of Father's own brilliant creation, each like a facet of a diamond showing part of God's image.

Destiny in their name:

- Eph 3:14, 15: "For this reason I bow my knees before the Father, from whom every (or "the whole") family in heaven and on earth derives its name"

This passage introduces the idea that "family" here includes the generations gone before, no longer on earth. And "family" is "patria" in the original language, meaning ancestral family lineage – this verse addresses *who we come from* and says that Father God has caused this lineage to have a name.

The passage makes clear that the family or clan name is not merely a random set of phonemes, codes or sounds. That name has a divine intentionality hidden in the time and location he placed our people and tied to intentional destiny.

> That name reflects two separate and important streams that flow around the "island of us":
> - One stream of that name reflects the process of our groping to find Him
> - The other stream of purpose is a reflection of Father's secret and brilliant idea for our destiny as a clan or lineage

The secret of Babel is this. What God set in motion there is not a *curse* but *a recovery*, hidden in the deep wisdom of God are three brilliant principles:

1. The original plan was that people would live with Father and would manage the earth to the place where its beauty and bounty most reflected Father's generous and joyful nature. This would result in each person experiencing their giftedness and contribution in a place of plenty. He is bringing his children back to that place and destiny but with even more glory and fellowship.

2. But having rejected that original purpose and having broken fellowship with God, mankind was influenced by evil and sought to supplant God forever at Babel. And that disaster was potentially even worse in scope and consequence than the entrance of death into the world because it would give the evil one access to heaven in new ways.

3. And so Father set into motion a force that would carry us across the face of the globe and there he secretly set in our path things that would cause us to long for him, longing to return to Eden and to our Father. He built this longing into the codes of the sunsets and movement of the planets, into giving birth, and into our deaths, and into family, language, and culture – and even in our stories ("...He has also set eternity in their heart..." Ecc 3:11) And his intention was beautiful, that we would not only seek him and find him but that we would understand his brilliant idea and destiny for each one of us. That is what it means when it says that for each of us he has set into motion a "name" of his choosing.

In our groping to find him, in the place and time he sets us, by finding him we find not only a return to Eden and a return to fellowship with our true Father, but we find a door into destiny. That is, the very beautiful, creative and brilliant idea he had for our fathers and our clan to live in. His loving intention is that clans and families find out how to live that destiny for the world. That destiny grows up from the soil of our restored fellowship with him, in the very place and time he has set us. So our name and our clan and the place and time of our people are an important part of how we both enter into restored fellowship with Father and into a restoration to our path of destiny, what our clan brings to life in the world.

This beautiful destiny was not revoked or removed from the people but delayed. We read in the bible that in eternity there stand around the throne (Rev 7:9) persons from every (each) of the nations, peoples, clans, languages, dialects, and ethnicities. And we infer that it was his intention to bring each of these streams to the throne for his purpose, each carrying in their uniqueness a special aspect that reflects a part of Father's investment in mankind of his own image. This reflection gives glory to God by making that special aspect of his character or glory visible like a diamond separating the spectrum of light.

Sometimes a people or clan stumble and fail to come into their destiny in the land that the Lord has placed them in. Sometimes the Lord has placed different peoples, clans, and tribes together. In his wisdom he intends then that they should seek their destiny together, that they should be restored to the path of destiny over the land together.

The Culture of Heaven And The Destiny of Peoples

As Father creates a restored connection with himself, he does this simply for the joy of reconnection and fellowship. However, it is his pleasure also to guide them in the Holy Spirit to be restored to the destiny he has for the people placed on this land. And there is a priority or precedence that is tied to the original people he set on the land, because theirs was the original destiny which the Lord has never revoked, revealed in the land and in the name.

I strongly believe, in order that America can find its true destiny in God, native peoples and immigrants (including those brought here originally by force), must seek Father together if we are to find it.

Something good is happening:

One day a pastor friend of mine and I were on a spiritual adventure, taking a day to just follow the Holy Spirit. We were led to a place near an old fort where two rivers meet. When we stood on the land I could see the "blood on the land", although I had never learned its history. But clear as day I could see a stockade and many women and children starving inside, and many who had died. I later learned this was precisely what had happened on that spot, one sad result of the US-Dakota War.

Some other friends I know held a special meeting called "The Dakota Honoring". This was a very special event that I think Father planned. You may know that in the 1860's some very greedy people withheld food, blankets, and money from Dakota people and many starved. It was a clear breach of promises and treaties. Breaching covenants is one of the things that creates "blood on the land" (see Isa 24:5,6).

When the greedy people withheld food and blankets and people started starving, conflict broke out, mostly just to get food for people. It quickly got really ugly. The Dakota people were then removed from Minnesota (mostly), their ancestral homeland. These are sad historic facts. My friends wanted to honor all Dakota people and organized an event in the heart of their homeland, Mankato, Minnesota. Many people came to the honoring event, including many of the Dakota' kinsmen from Montana, Nebraska, Canada, North and South Dakota, and other places. The event was one for Dakota people to tell their stories and for all attending to attune to share grief together. There were other purposes, one was for repentance and the other, the most important, was to give heartfelt honor to Dakota people.

I had asked Minnesota's Governor to prepare a letter to Dakota people as an act of official repentance and as a prophetic act. Unexpectedly, the Governor's people had me write the letter. I think the Lord orchestrated this so that I was able to write the letter the way Jesus wanted it. The letter read:

Whereas the people of Mankato Minnesota, civic leaders, churches, and its citizens have organized Dakota Honor Gathering in order to welcome Dakota people to the State of Minnesota, their ancestral home;

Whereas we the people of the State of Minnesota hereby recognize the events of December 26, 1862 and carry in our hearts a deeply heartfelt sorrow for the loss of life that occurred in these events and the days that followed;

Whereas we are looking together as a State for a new day which can equally be celebrated by peoples of all races, tribes, and language groups;

Now therefore, I, Mark Dayton, Governor of the State of Minnesota, hereby proclaim this day, May 25th, 2017 as the "Dakota Honoring Day". I therefore proclaim on the behalf of the people of Minnesota, "yahdipi kiŋ waśte!", "welcome home".

How joyfully the words "welcome home" were received by the people.

Providentially, the mayors of two cities involved in the Dakota Honoring also asked me to draft their letters. Their proclamation was also prophetic. By that I mean, God helped me write them. Here is what was said:

> Together the people of Mankato and North Mankato, Minnesota hereby proclaim:
>
> Whereas, the beautiful plains that we all call home are more blessed when we live together, acknowledging people from every race, tongue, and tribe, and valuing the presence of all people, native and non-native.
>
> Whereas we together acknowledge that this sense of blessing has not always been present. Wars, tragedies, prejudice, injustices, and other sorrowful events have marred this land in the past. This is especially true of the dark days of what has been called "the US/Dakota War" and the days that followed. We acknowledge the pain and loss that occurred at the time. We acknowledge particularly that a great injustice was done when the Dakota people were expelled by force from the State, which

The Culture of Heaven And The Destiny of Peoples

had been for generations the homeland of the Dakota people. The people of our region reject the prejudice of the past and turn back and turn away from this prejudice and welcome a new day, where this community welcomes and celebrates the people of all races, tribes, and language groups.

Now therefore, we, Eric Anderson, Mayor of the City of Mankato, and Mark Dehen, Mayor of the City of North Mankato, in the State of Minnesota proclaim that the time is "ripe" for reconciliation, not denying the past but seeking mutual forgiveness and healing, together, native and non-native. And in this spirit, we, on behalf of Mankato and North Mankato, Minnesota proclaim this day May 25, 2017 as "Dakota Honoring Day." We together say on behalf of the people of Mankato and North Mankato, say, "yahdipi kiŋ waśte!", "welcome home."

I think that the Lord visited this and other Dakota honoring events. I want to share something very special that happened. There is a pastor named Jamey VanGelder. I honor him as a man of God. He asked someone, "how do you honor Dakota people?" and he was told to give them a Pendleton Blanket. This is important because Pendleton blankets were promised to Dakota people before winter and were not given to them. This was another reason the war happened. So he found one. The blanket design was of an elder pointing up to the stars, surrounded by children. He kept the blanket in his church prayer room, thinking that someday he would know what to do with it. Jamey had played a part in the Wokiksuye Ride or 38+2 Ride held each year, when it first started in 2005. This was an important part of honoring Dakota people. This ride has been going on for years but Jamey had not been actively going. The event is held on Dec 26 each year, the day the Dakota men were hung. On Christmas night Jamey had a dream of going to Mankato, to a church that supports the event with meals and a welcoming and honoring atmosphere (the same church that hosted the Dakota Honoring). In the dream he saw himself speaking to the gathering. In the morning Jamey's wife, when she heard the dream, urged him to go to Mankato and he did. When Pastor Jamey walked into the dinner event, around 300 Dakota people were there. Jamey stood at the back to watch the event. But the pastor of that church saw him and invited him to speak. Without any prepared plan to speak, Jamey asked the Lord to help him as he took the microphone. He spoke into the destiny of Dakota people, in their land and in their name. Then he felt called to give the blanket. But he had no idea who to give it to among the 300 gathered. The person on his left and right also had no idea, so asking God for help, Jamey selected someone his eyes were drawn toward, almost randomly. He asked the man to come to receive the blanket. When the blanket was revealed the whole crowd grew intensely quiet. Something obviously miraculous had happened. The man Jamey had called forward was the one man among all the family of Sioux tribes appointed to teach the stars to the next generation. The hand of God was unmistakable, and it powerfully witnessed to the message Jamey had shared. It was God's thumbprint.

I believe the Lord himself is longing for and calling for a year in which the church in North America call urgently on him for blessings on each of the original people's of America. This is not a call for "revival" but a call for *blessing*. We can separately call on the Lord for revival. But I believe that the Lord will *hear a call for revival* out of a call to him for restoration and blessing. It is a matter of justice. It is a matter of blood that is on the land that is cleansed by justice.

When we call for revival first, and not blessing first, our hearts can have mixed motives. When we call unreservedly on the Lord for blessing, our hearts are more like his own heart. He wants us to have hearts like his toward people. Jesus said, "so that you may be sons of your Father who is in heaven; for He causes His sun to rise on the evil and the good, and sends rain on the righteous and the unrighteous... Therefore you are to be perfect, as your heavenly Father is perfect."

I believe if people call on the Lord unreservedly for blessing, he will hear this call as if it was a call for revival. It will bring every blessing on people until they are able to live in the beautiful destiny and dream Father has for them in their land, until they are very beautiful and shine.

For America to understand the destiny Father first dreamt over the land, its first peoples must lead in the seeking, but with all of us together. Sons and daughters of every tribe are meant to reveal to creation the beautiful dream Father has for people and by doing so, his glory begins to fill the earth.

As the Lord reveals to us sonship and kingdom family, as we see Father's joyful heart and beautiful dream for every tribe, our human prejudice is "plowed up". That is, the act of knowing the beauty of Father's heart "overturns" our hardness and selfishness and the soil of our heart becomes truly fertile. This is a wonderfully pure expression of the culture of heaven.

For many believers in the world, the areas where are hearts may be hardened is toward the sons of Ishmael. How we need Father to plow under the hard places of our heart. We may be especially hard hearted toward Islamic people because we feel fear because of terrorism. But Jesus is about to do something amazing. A time of extraordinary harvest is coming to the house of Ishmael. We need to have our hearts ready, clean from hatred, plowed from prejudice. The church must be ready to let love for the other house of Abraham manifest in the language of love, love in action.

We must joyfully and without reservation love these people in order to build a spiritual path for them to return to Father in Jesus. The destiny of Ishmael is critical to the close of history. The church must awake to a spirit of intercession over Ishmael's sons if we are to "hasten the day of the Lord."

Faisal Malick, a dear pastor and brother from Pakistan said wisely, "We need to abandon our perspectives in favor of the heartbeat of heaven. We need to understand that there is a special endtime purpose for the sons of Islam. We need to awaken a deeply buried cry in the heart of muslim people." Pastor Malick also said, "the name 'Ishmael' means 'God hears' and his name is his primary destiny, a divine appointment. The well that God caused to spring up supernaturally in the desert to keep Hagar and Ishmael alive is a prophetic statement that God has a divine love and purpose for Ishmael." The sons of Ishmael are those primarily chosen to "provoke Israel to jealousy" as they experience the abiding "shekina glory", miracles, and the beautiful presence of God.

As the Lord has pulled away my human prejudice, I have found myself eager to have muslim friends, to fast with them during Ramadan, to share Jesus just naturally as he is so much a part of my life.

Our hearts are meant to be "perfect" as our Father's heart. We must learn to see as he sees and love as he loves. Ask Father to reveal himself to you in a way that first "wins your heart" to himself, because of his own beauty, and then transforms your heart to be like his own.

Father frequently asks me to realign my heart and perspective to his. Sometimes this is a painful process but it always yields a beauty and a cleanness that is delightfully sweet. It is core to the culture of heaven.

One thing to take away is this, that critical to becoming enculturated to heaven's culture is to allow him to give us a heart like Jesus, to allow him to plow up our human prejudice. This means that we do not hold on tightly to our opinions and we are quick to exchange our view for his. In fact, this is critical. We are meant to align with his eternal purposes for all the people of the earth. It begins with having his heart and sharing his dream for each person, family, and clan. This is the foundation. But what must follow is sharing with him his dream in ways it manifests in prayer, intercession, and obedient engagement. That "obedient engagement" is this: we are children, uncomplicated and simple, whose aim is simply to be obedient to what he shows us to do. When we do what he says, in the manner of his heart, glory and beauty appears on the earth, "as in heaven so on earth".

Chapter 6

The Glory of Father God in the Church, His Glory in the Saints

O f all of the birthrights of Jesus the firstborn, the most beautiful and precious is that of the presence of his Father wherever he went. Jesus was securely attached to Father and lived in the continual cycle of always pleasing Father and sharing life together with him. This is a very virtuous cycle of joy. Think of this, *a relationship* changed the world. Although joyful fellowship is an end in itself, Jesus' fellowship with his Father changed the entire destiny of the world and its peoples, including you and me.

For the family of God, living in the close of history, we are called as little children to cooperate with Father in some very important things. The part that each of us play is simple. We are to be like small children, holding the hand of our Father walking through a busy station. Our only job is to keep our attention on him, hold onto his hand, and follow.

As our savior Jesus continues to reveal Father (as he has throughout history, and most importantly, in his earthly life and ministry) and as Holy Spirit shows us Father in such intimate and tender ways, the church is on the brink of becoming a glory and a light such as we have never known.

I think it's important to understand that this glory, this sweet, powerful presence is native to the church. It is it's natural state. Scripture speaks very directly to this. In the verses below we see that it is the will and intention of God that his presence and glory be manifest in His church and that this manifestation be in ways that are transformative to the church and the world. It is our birthright as co-heirs of Jesus.

In the history of modern revivals there are thousands of examples of each of these manifestations. In many of the great outbreaks of revival there have been tremendous miracles. In the outbreak of revival in Indonesia, Tanzania, and in the Azusa Street revivals, visible fire filled churches.

A friend of mine, an accountant in Tanzania, manning a mission station while the missionaries were away, was visited by representatives of a tribe. They had walked many days from their village to ask an important question. That was, "we have read in the book about many miracles and we wonder if these are for today?"

My friend said simply, "yes". They then asked, "then how do we receive them?" My friend said, "you ask". The representatives from the village were overjoyed and returned to their village with great anticipation. The believers gathered to hear the news and when they heard, "you ask" they did so, gathered in their grass roof church. Within minutes the village bell was ringing and the villagers gathered buckets of water and ran to the church which was engulfed in intense fire, only to find the church filled with people, worshiping, crying, speaking in other languages, and full of intense joy in fellowship with Father. Similarly, the revival in Indonesia fell with fire in the small town of Soe (you can read about this in "Like A Mighty Wind" or my favorite, "The Gentle Breeze of Jesus" by Mel Tari...).

Similarly, according to newspaper reports, the Los Angeles Fire Department received frequent fire calls to the Azusa Street church when revival broke out there because witnesses could see fire on the building or its roof. In one account, people calling the Fire Department were told "we get many calls to this place, please go check again."

Recorded instances of clouds of glory, intense and beautiful light, visitations of angels, and other manifestations number in the many hundreds. This is actually the normal state of the church in the simple sense that scriptures declare: (a) glory is the native state of the church, of its essence (see the scripture references that follow); (b) the Lord Jesus said that he himself would gather with us and be among us.

Scripture is clear about Father's intention that his glory be in the church. Some of these scripture speak about the glory that is being revealed now but will be so fully manifest in the future, in eternity. But some of the verses below clearly reveal that this eternal manifestation of glory has an important, present, and immediate manifestation. Some of these verses speak to the future and some speak to the present. Scripture is very clear about both the future and present glory of the church.

In this section, the verses that follow primarily speak of the "true nature" of the church and of its glory, God's glory manifest in the church. There are many verses listed here and I encourage you to read through all of these or pick some that stand out to you.

This first group of verses tell us that God's glory is present in the church by its essential nature but indicate that this will be more clearly seen in the future:

1. Romans 5:2: "through whom also we have obtained our introduction by faith into this grace in which we stand; and we exult in **hope of the glory of God**" (the term "hope" indicates that the verse speaks to a *coming* glory).
2. Romans 8:18: "For I consider that the sufferings of this present time are not worthy to be

compared with the **glory that is to be revealed to us**" (a *coming* glory to be revealed).

3. Romans 9:23: "And He did so to make *known* the riches of **His glory upon vessels of mercy, which He prepared beforehand for glory**" (this speaks of a glory that is both future and present, known now and more fully known in the next age. This revelation is not only made to the church, but also to the spiritual realm, see also Eph 3:10).

4. 1 Peter 1:7: "so that the proof of your faith, being more precious than gold which is perishable, even though tested by fire, may be found to result in praise and **glory** and honor at the revelation of Jesus Christ". See also: 1Peter 5:4: "And when the Chief Shepherd appears, you will receive **the unfading crown of glory**" (these two verses indicate a fullness of the revelation of glory for the church at Jesus' second coming).

5. Similarly, Ephesians 5:27: "that He might present to Himself the church **in all her glory, having no spot or wrinkle or any such thing; but that she would be holy and blameless**" (future and now). See also Colossians 3:4 "When Christ, who is our life, is revealed, then you also will be revealed with Him **in glory**" (future and now).

6. We see this in living color in Revelations 21: 2,11,23: "And I saw the holy city, new Jerusalem, coming down out of heaven from God, made

> ready as a bride adorned for her husband. And he carried me away in the Spirit to a great and high mountain, and showed me the holy city, Jerusalem, coming down out of heaven from God, **having the glory of God**. Her brilliance was like a very costly stone, as a stone of crystal-clear jasper. And the city has no need of the sun or of the moon to shine on it, **for the glory of God has illumined it**, and its lamp is the Lamb."

Scripture is perhaps surprisingly quite clear about God's intention that the church experience glory in the present age as well. Many of the scriptures here speak of both the future and present glory of the church but do so in a way that indicates that this state has a current manifestation in the church in this age. I encourage you to read all of these verses but if there are too many, pick ones that stand out to you. Regardless, I have highlighted certain parts of the verses that you can pay special attention to:

1. Romans 8:21: "that the creation itself also will be set free from its slavery to corruption into the **freedom of the glory of the children of God**. (Present tense for the children of God, seen in the freedom that is ours in Christ" (this freedom flows from a revelation that we are true, secure children of Father).

2. Romans 9:23: "And He did so to make known the riches of **His glory upon vessels of mercy, which He prepared beforehand for glory**" (In the context of this verse it is his glory being seen in his children even in their weaknesses and faults as their personal Father God supports them through the trials Paul describes).
3. 1 Corinthians 2:7: "but we speak God's wisdom in a mystery, the hidden wisdom which God predestined before the ages **to our glory**" (the mystery, the wisdom of God manifests in our glory).
4. 2 Corinthians 3:8,9: "**how will the ministry of the Spirit fail to be even more with glory**? For if the ministry of condemnation has glory, much more does the ministry of righteousness **abound in glory**" (God's glory is seen in simple believers in the ministry of reconciliation with God).
5. 2 Corinthians 3:18: "But we all, with unveiled face, beholding as in a mirror the glory of the Lord, are being transformed into the same image from **glory to glory**, just as from the Lord, the Spirit" (the glory seen in believers as they *change* and *transform* in life in the eyes of the people around them).
6. 1 Peter 1:8: "and though you have not seen Him, you love Him, and though you do not see Him now, but believe in Him, you greatly rejoice

with **joy inexpressible and full of glory**" (the glory seen on the saints by the world in the joy we have in believing and in our trust and faith).

7. 1 Peter 4:14: "If you are reviled for the name of Christ, you are blessed, **because the Spirit of glory and of God rests on you**" (in its context, it is the glory being seen while believers suffer persecution).

8. 2 Corinthians 4:6: "For God, who said, "Light shall shine out of darkness," is the One who has shone in our hearts to give the Light of the knowledge of **the glory of God in the face of Christ**" (the glory of God seen in his people who experience his light and freedom).

9. Ephesians 1:18: "I pray that the eyes of your heart may be enlightened, so that you will know what is the hope of His calling, what are the **riches of the glory** of His inheritance in the saints" (Father's glory seen in his people as they have revelation of his sweet mercies)

10. Ephesians 5:27: "that He might present to Himself the church in **all her glory**, having no spot or wrinkle or any such thing; but that she would be holy and blameless" (future and now, the glory of the church in holiness and in their whole devotion to Jesus)

11. Colossians 1:27: "to whom God willed to make known what is the riches of the glory of this mystery among the Gentiles, which is Christ in

you**, the hope of glory**" (the glory that Christ lives among his people).
12. 1 Thessalonians 2:12: "so that you would walk in a manner worthy of the God who calls you into His own kingdom and **glory**" (glory seen by non-believers as they see the power of God helping us walk in a way even beyond our human strength to walk, even in persecution, trials of life)
13. 2 Thessalonians 2:14: "It was for this He called you through our gospel, that you may gain **the glory of our Lord Jesus Christ**".
14. 2 Timothy 2:10: "For this reason I endure all things for the sake of those who are chosen, so that they also may obtain the salvation which is in Christ Jesus and with it **eternal glory**".
15. Hebrews 2:10: "For it was fitting for Him, for whom are all things, and through whom are all things, in bringing many sons **to glory**, to perfect the author of their salvation through sufferings" (again, glory seen in his people even in their suffering).

The glory of God in the church is simply the manifestation of his beauty, character, and attributes through his living presence among his people. The glory is like a stream flowing down from the fountain of Jesus and his genuine presence among us. It manifests in many ways and forms but always as a reflection of his glory (like the moon reflecting the sun, sometimes so brightly in the night). This glory manifests so naturally when we are connected with him. It manifests in ways such as:

- Awe (see Acts 2:43, below)
- Signs and Wonders (so natural for Jesus)
- Fear of the Lord leading to holiness

See Acts 2:43: "Everyone kept feeling a sense of awe; and many wonders and signs were taking place through the apostles" (we see this repeated also in Acts 4:24-33 and Acts 5:12-16). This glory was manifest in:

- Joy in intense, beautiful fellowship with Father and people – as we enter into Jesus' own love from Father (true sonship, see John 17:26, 1 John 1:3)
- Joyful Liberty as sons, true sonship (see 2 Cor 3:17 and Rom 8:21)

Scripture describes the presence of glory and of God in the church as the normal state of the church. The current state which is dominated by human works is a diminished state. Glory manifested in awe, fear, holiness, miracles, and exceeding joy in fellowship are the normal state.

The visitation of God, leading to his habitation among us, changes us. Let's look at this first from

Exodus and the tent of meeting where God's presence and glory were intensely manifest:

- Exodus 29:43-46: "I will meet there with the sons of Israel, **and it shall be consecrated by My glory**. I will consecrate the tent of meeting and the altar; I will also consecrate Aaron and his sons to minister as priests to Me. I will dwell among the sons of Israel and will be their God. They shall know that I am the LORD their God who brought them out of the land of Egypt, that I might dwell among them; I am the LORD their God."

The Lord is intending in this passage, to visit the tent of meeting with his own presence and glory, in cloud and fire. And that glory overwhelms all human aspects of the tent of meeting like a wave rolling over a stone at the shore, totally changing the character and nature of the simple construction of man with intense, and beautiful holiness. We need his transformative glory and presence to come and consecrate our gatherings:

- 2 Cor 3:18 says, "But we all, with unveiled face, beholding as in a mirror the glory of the lord, are being transformed into the same image from glory to glory, just as by the Spirit of the Lord"

As Father is revealed to us and then through us, and his true character is made known, it will be a great glory to him and to his church. It will manifest in signs and wonders but the glory of the miraculous will be far out-stripped by the glory of his *nature* being seen in us. This is Father's intention for his people at this time in history, and he is beginning to manifest it everywhere.

Over the last 100 years, as Jesus has been giving his church revelation to prepare her for the times that are now coming upon us, we have seen him restore "essentials" to his church. The revelation of a personal connection with Jesus, the fellowship and power of the Holy Spirit are two of these. In this time in church history Christ is "dressing" or "gowning" his bride with sonship and glory.

There are many ways we have seen this glory manifest. Sometimes it takes a form that is visible to some or all of the persons present in a place where he manifests his presence. People have often seen a cloud fill a room, reminding us of the glory that filled Solomon's temple, or the cloud hovering over the tent of meeting, or of Isaiah's vision in the temple of the Lord. On some occasions a tangible scent of roses fills a room, even large rooms, and holy awe touches everyone there, reminding us of the presence of the rose of Sharon. In some cases the light in a place suddenly becomes overwhelmingly bright and a deep and holy awe fills everyone present. In these tangible cases and in many cases where there is no visible manifestation of glory there may be sudden and spontaneous healings on many person's present, with no one praying. Often these times are silent or people sing spontaneously in unison in songs they have never learned. A sense of holy awe comes upon people.

I believe that the manifest presence of the risen Lord Jesus is the native state of the church and when Jesus said that he would be present with us ("where two or more are gathered", Matt 18:19,20) we must take this with great seriousness.

At this time the risen Lord Jesus wants to reveal himself *into* the church, into our gatherings in a way that is unique in history because we are stepping over a threshold in time where his bride greatly needs him by their side to sustain us through times of significant pressure. But it is not meant to be merely a sustaining act but an act to beautify, to glorify, to thrill his people at his dear presence. And he intends, as he has always intended as a core aspect of his mission, to reveal Father to us. Father's kisses will be greatly sustaining to us in the days just ahead.

We see in the Bible that many times when the presence of God became manifest among people that there were tangible manifestations of various sorts. Here are some examples:

The most common manifestation of his presence in scripture is a spontaneous appearance of fire:

- Ex 19:18 – fire on the mountain
- Ex 24:17 – fire on the mountain
- Num 16:35 – fire from the presence of the Lord

- 2 King 1:10 – Elijah and the company
- Ex 3:2 – a burning bush
- 1 Chron 20:36 – fire falling on David's sacrifice after the plague
- 2 Chron 7:1 – fire falling on Solomon's alter
- 1 Kings 18:38 – fire falling on Elijah's sacrifice
- Ex 13:21-23; Ex 14:19 - fire by night cloud of fire by day
- Acts 2:2-4 – fire appearing on each one

Another manifestation that the Bible often clearly identifies specifically associated with the presence of "the glory" of God is a cloud, sometimes called a "Cloud of Glory":

- Ex 40:34 – the cloud descends and the glory of the Lord fills the tabernacle
- Ex 40:35 – the Glory of the Lord filled the tabernacle in the form of cloud
- 2 Chron 5:14 and I Kings 8:10,11 - Cloud of Glory in the temple
- Ex 16:10 – the glory of the Lord appeared in the cloud
- Num 16:42 – the cloud covered the tent of meeting and the glory appeared
- Ezek 10:4 – cloud fills the temple as glory fills
- Ezek 44:4 – The glory fills the house of the Lord
- Isa 4:5 – promise that the cloud and flame will cover the whole of Mount Zion

- Lev 16:2 – promise that "I will appear in the cloud over the mercy seat"

Bright Light:
- Ezek 43: 2-5 – bright light as glory fills the temple
- Acts 9:3-20 – Saul on the road to Damascus

Dove:
- John 1:32 and Matt 3:16 – dove appears as the Holy Spirit descends

Visitations:
- Dan 3:24 – 4th man in the furnace

Wind:
- Acts 2:2-4 – the audible wind

Signs and wonders, healing and miracles are also a constant sign of the presence of the Lord and are often also a spontaneous manifestation of His presence. In that sense of course, Jesus, Emmanuel, "God with us" is the obvious example, unrivalled in its importance. This Glory was always on Jesus as Son of Man.

The phenomenon of manifestations are not critical, nor even important, really, but the *presence* is important. In that sense, perhaps the manifestations *are* important, in that they could possibly serve to "gauge" the level of the intensity of the presence of the Lord we are experiencing. My concern in dismissing the importance of "manifestations of his presence" this is simply that we have become accustomed to our current "normal", a "tepid temperature" and "low-intensity atmosphere". For that reason alone I would encourage us to seek a new hunger and a new level of faith and expectation, even to open the door to these manifestations. They are unquestionably biblical. That is, there are clear biblical precedents for all of the manifestations we are describing. That should be enough for us to hunger for them.

My wife Adri and I have often experienced the presence and glory of the Lord. One time Adri was praying very urgently over something, really seeking the Lord, and a cloud appeared all around her. Our youngest son was so amazed to see it but he didn't know what it was or what was happening and needed us to tell him it was the sweet presence of the Lord. One time in Indonesia, although our ministry was going great, especially prophetic ministry, I was personally feeling very depressed. Some things were really hard for us. When Adri prayed for me, the room was suddenly filled with a bright and very intense light. Adri immediately went on her face in the fear of the Lord. I laid back in the light and asked the Holy Spirit to go into every corner of my memories, affections, conscious and unconscious mind, and speak the truth to me. When we used to prayer walk in some neighborhoods in Indonesia, especially ones that had a strong Jihadi presence, I would ask Jesus to walk with me and Father to receive the walk as an incense. In those walks, especially in the darkest places, I often felt tangible fire on me, especially on my fingers where the turbulent air flowed hotly between them. I think there are many experiences like this that we could share - how we treasure each of them!

Of course, what we hunger for is simply the beauty of the Lord Jesus present among us in all of the surprising and beautiful ways he comes. We know that the manifestations themselves are NOT the presence. But to accommodate our own nature, our preference for our "current normal", we need to kick the door open and leave it open. A certain few of us may be too excited by the manifestation and not treasure the beauty of the presence. For these, maybe they need more of the "still, small voice". But most of us may be too comfortable living in the confines of our own constructions, comfortable with the tepid temperature of our current experience. For most of us, a new hunger must take hold and break the hold of our current normal until we become wildly hungry for his presence and for breakthrough.

It is truly the birthright of the church to host the presence of the Lord, the living Lord Jesus, Father, and Holy Spirit. It is a manifestation of the culture of heaven in our gatherings - and I think heaven is hungry to invade us.

Chapter 7

Stirring the Passions of the Almighty

Sons and daughters pray differently than slaves and orphans. As Jesus shares his birthrights with us, it includes intimate access to Father. Access by children to Father's heart exists because it reflects Father's core values, it reflects his personal culture and the culture of heaven.

We often do not ask the primary question about prayer. We often "do" prayer as a Christian discipline. Prayer is something "the Christian 'does'". We are looking for growth. We are looking to fulfill a spiritual discipline that will benefit our walk with God. However, we rarely ask *what is happening with God*?

Secondarily, we often think of God as a mysterious, powerful, wise being and we wonder, if we are brutally honest with ourselves, whether we are *able* to understand the mystery of his will, can we ever really understand his infinite thoughts about a matter and pray accordingly? What does prayer matter if we don't know really how to *move* God?

In this section I want to share a little about how God describes himself, how he is ***a person*** whose heart can be touched, his feelings and passions enflamed into action, his mind changed by the movements of his own heart. I think you will see how this changes our posture of prayer, it changes the nature of *effective prayer*.

There is a profound difference when sons and daughters intercede compared with slaves and orphans because sons and daughters have access to Abba's heart. As they access his heart as only dear children can do, they enter into a capacity to stir the passions of God. We are seeing this as we are understanding more from God about our birthrights as sons and daughters.

First I want you to consider what God says about himself, about the stirrings of his heart. Consider the following scriptures:

Father's heart can be moved; his heart can be stirred:

- Isa 63:15 (NASB) — Look down from heaven and see from Your holy and glorious habitation; Where are Your zeal and Your mighty deeds? *The stirrings of Your heart and Your compassion* are restrained toward me.

Isaiah is revealing here how God moves in mighty deeds because his heart is stirred. The prophet also understands that it is natural that God's heart moves toward us *unless* something is blocking it. We are to pray in the understanding that his own compassions move him!

- Hos 11:8 – *God is speaking and it shows the nature of his heart*:
  How can I give you up, O Ephraim?
  How can I surrender you, O Israel?
  How can I make you like Admah?
  How can I treat you like Zeboiim?
  My heart is turned over within Me, All My compassions are kindled.

Think about that, how God's compassions stir in his heart. Children have access to these parts of the heart of God and that is how we learn to pray, by tuning in to these. But just to be certain that we understand each other, I am saying it is simple, not saying it is easy. There is often a breaking that happens within us as we become attuned to what's happening in Father. Remember that "in the same way the Spirit also helps our weakness; for we do not know how to pray as we should, but the Spirit Himself intercedes for us with groanings too deep for words" (Rom 8:26).

What that may mean is that we have to begin understanding how to pray as we ought by joining the

Holy Spirit in groaning, attuning to the burden God is carrying about a matter. If we make ourselves vulnerable to be with him at a heart level, sharing his concern, abandoning our perspective and prejudice, we can start to become a little like him. Then we can pray from the place that draws on the stirrings of his heart.

We know little about Jesus "prayer life" as in "what did he say to Father". We know that he was in constant fellowship with Father. We know he spent some nights apart from his friends, in order to deeply pray. But when Jesus went to raise Lazarus, he also was deeply moved and groaned and was troubled. In John 11:33 and 38 we read about this. I think this was Jesus tuning into Father and Holy Spirit and you could call it praying in a way.

When I was younger I was very spiritually ambitious because I was forming my identity and subconsciously I thought that spiritual things could be a good basis for loving myself. I had not learned much about Father's heart yet. I had an audacious idea. Each month I would pray through the church roster. I would rock this church because I would pray harder and more sincerely than anyone. I started on the first person in the roster. About 20 minutes into it I said, "Jesus, I don't feel that you are really listening". The response I sensed was something like, "were you talking to me?" And I said, "of course I am talking to you, I am praying". Silence. Then I asked why he was not listening. He gently asked if I want to know. I knew there was "trouble" coming. But I wanted to know.

And he told me that in my heart I had the wrong perspective toward the woman I was praying for. I did not like how shy she was, excessively shy in my view. She would hardly speak if there were more than two people around. He told me that he made her on purpose and he loved her the way she was. So I repented of seeing her that way. I repented until I felt clean and humble. Then I started praying again for her and still found Jesus "not listening". I was frustrated and ask him again. He asked me if I wanted to know. This time he showed me that I was judging her for being so skinny, eating only "healthy foods" and making the rest of us look bad, and so on. He said again that he made her on purpose the way she was. So I repented again.

Now I am 90 minutes into my prayer for the first person on the list and have not even really prayed. But I felt beautifully clean. Actually, before this experience I had no real idea of how Jesus himself was feeling. Then I waited on Jesus, to see if my heart was like his, and if I could pray. Instantly five things, very specific things, came to my mind to pray for. I prayed these but was kind of exhausted. The next Sunday, my friend stopped the church service in order to speak. So much for her being "shy". She said, "this week God did five things in my life..." and named the very things I had prayed for. Being "with" him in his heart when we pray is so essential.

I think we start by attuning to his heart, drawing upon his compassion, having our hearts made more like his, then we receive from the Spirit the mind of

Christ, his strategies and purposes. It is a safety to us because it keeps us childlike and humble to pray this way. Our own agendas are shortsighted and need to be exchanged for his.

Children can pray this way. They can access their Abba's heart - and stir his compassions. But I think it starts as Jesus said, that we become converted and humble as children in order to bring our hearts to this place. Here is an example of God's heart in motion, what we can join:

- Jer 31:20 "Is Ephraim My dear son? Is he a delightful child? Indeed, as often as I have spoken against him, I certainly still *remember* him; Therefore *My heart yearns for him*; I will surely have mercy on him," declares the LORD.

EXAMPLES of his heart in action:
The God who sings love songs:
- Zeph 3:17 The Lord your God is in your midst, a mighty one who will save; he will rejoice over you with gladness; he will quiet you by his love; he will exult (giyl) over you with loud singing.

"Giyl" in Hebrew describes joy so great that it *spontaneously causes one to dance, leap, exult*. Culturally some of us may not have seen that modeled for us. But it is spontaneous, joyful, flowing right from his heart. He does not change. He is still like that.

The God who rejoices, who throws parties (lost sheep, lost coin):
- Luke 15:7 "I tell you that in the same way, there will be more joy in heaven over one sinner who repents than over ninety-nine righteous persons who need no repentance."
- Luke 15: 10 "In the same way, I tell you, there is joy in the presence of the angels of God over one sinner who repents."
- Luke 15: 15:32 'But we had to celebrate and rejoice, for this brother of yours was dead and has begun to live, and was lost and has been found.'"

He brings to remembrance:
Themes:
Bringing things to God's mind (examples and commands)
- Example of Solomon in 2 Chron 1:9 – Solomon reminds God of his promises
- Example of Jehosophat in 2 Chron 20:7-9 – Jehosophat reminds God of his promises
- In Isa 43:26 God challenges us to do this with "put me in remembrance"
- David models this in Psa 25:6 "Remember, O LORD, Your compassion and Your lovingkindnesses, for they have been from of old."
- Isa 62:6-8 "On your walls, O Jerusalem, I have appointed watchmen; all day and all night they will never keep silent. You who remind the LORD, take no rest for yourselves; and give

Him no rest until He establishes and makes Jerusalem a praise in the earth".

When we speak about "putting God in remembrance" we are not describing an act of bringing up the terms of a contract but instead we are speaking of an act of deliberately activating the very compassions of the heart of God.

When God brings things in remembrance this moves him. It is a deliberate act because something has moved his heart.

- 1 Cor 2:10,11 For to us God revealed them through the Spirit; for the Spirit searches all things, even the depths of God. For who among men knows the thoughts of a man except the spirit of the man which is in him? Even so the thoughts of God no one knows except the Spirit of God.

Jesus and Holy Spirit are advocates within the Godhead. They advocate not only for us but for God's own compassions.

EXAMPLES of Gods heart being provoked:
1) God's heart can be provoked to passionate remembrance of his love and mercy, of his covenant and promise;
2) God's heart can be provoked in his zeal and jealousy - and provoking the jealousy of God is a bad idea:

- 1 Cor 10:22 "Or do we provoke the Lord to jealousy? We are not stronger than He, are we?"
- James 4:5 "Or do you think that the Scripture speaks to no purpose: 'He jealously desires the Spirit which He has made to dwell in us'"?

His heart is close to each of us:
- Isa 63:9 – "In all their affliction He was afflicted, And the angel of His presence saved them; In His love and in His mercy He redeemed them, And He lifted them and carried them all the days of old".

His jealousy is *about* restoration:
- Hos 11:10 (his jealous zeal) "They will walk after the LORD, He will roar like a lion; Indeed He will roar And His sons will come trembling from the west".

When our hearts become like His and we share his passions it stirs **his** passions even more, it amplifies his urge to move.

His jealousy is not like the jealousy of man which is driven by covetousness, greed, and lust for what we want.

His jealousy is pure. It is driven from deep within his pure and intense love, the urge for justice, the passion for healing.

His jealousy does not result in his getting what he did not earn, it results in wholeness and restoration.

Father's jealousy is *protective jealousy*, not a predatory, controlling jealousy.

The nature of God:
- Exo 33:18,19 - Then Moses said, "I pray You, show me Your glory!" And He said, "I Myself will make all My goodness pass before you, and will proclaim the name of the LORD before you; and I will be gracious to whom I will be gracious, and will show compassion on whom I will show compassion."
- Eccles. 4:1 - Then I looked again at all the acts of oppression which were being done under the sun. And behold I saw the tears of the oppressed and that they had no one to comfort them; and on the side of their oppressors was power, but they had no one to comfort them.

Bill Johnson from Bethel Redding said in a message I heard, "It's much more fun to pray with God than merely to pray to Him." He then said, "God did not promise to answer our prayers once we learn to pray like robots. He actually makes Himself vulnerable to the desires of His people. This is easier to understand in sonship over servanthood."

How do we stir up the passions of God over ourselves, individually and corporately? How do we go about engaging with God such that we stir his passions, ignite his compassions in prayer?

1. Alignment with heaven's purposes. Alignment with heaven's culture. Alignment with the ways of God. When we begin to value his agenda and his perspective over our own.
2. More in the waiting, in the seeking, than in getting the prayers made into statements.
3. Faith, completely removing the issue of impossible from our mental vocabulary, and only seeking to know how he sees and praying in alignment with his wisdom and compassions.
4. We remove the space between what we are asking God to do and our willingness to be obedient. The act of asking and the act of moving become united, both in the prayer and following.
5. Being the intercessors that the Lord is waiting for, those who will pray "on earth as it is in heaven":
    a) "Our Father in Heaven, hallowed be Your name. Your kingdom come. Your will be done on earth as it is in Heaven." Matthew 6:9-10
    b) In both Isa 59:16 and 63:5 we see that God wondered and was "appalled" that there was no intercessor.

c) Father "seeking worshipers who will worship in spirit and truth" (John 4:24) – applied not only to the act of worship in singing, praising, but in joining our heart to his heart until we see from his perspective and join him in this place.

6. We bring to mind together what he has done for us, and draw it to his remembrance.

- Psa 12:5 "Because of the devastation of the afflicted, because of the groaning of the needy, now I will arise," says the LORD; "I will set him in the safety for which he longs."

- See Psalms 98 and 96, as we sing a new song to the Lord "he remembers his lovingkindness and faithfulness" (vs 3)

See Isa 42:10

> *Sing to the LORD a new song*, Sing His praise from the end of the earth!
> You who go down to the sea, and all that is in it. You islands, and those who dwell on them. Let the wilderness and its cities lift up their voices, The settlements where Kedar inhabits. Let the inhabitants of Sela sing aloud, Let them shout for joy from the tops of the mountains. Let them give glory to the LORD and declare His

> praise in the coastlands. The LORD will go forth like a warrior, *He will arouse His zeal* like a man of war. He will utter a shout, yes, he will raise a war cry. He will prevail against His enemies.

Learning to be sons and daughters, to have intimate access to the movements of his heart, is of the essence of the culture of heaven. Learning to partner with him in prayer by allowing our hearts to move to the rhythm of the movements of his heart is probably the most tender or intimate part of becoming true sons and daughters. It is certainly the best way we become enculturated to the culture of heaven.

Chapter 8

Removing a Heart of Stone and of Religion

I want to share with you two contrasting stories. Or you might say, one story that completes the other.

The first is this...my son had a friend who worked at one of the local satanist bookstores. She had been having really horrible night visitations, really tortuous. She asked her boss about what she should do and he said coldly, "you are dead". Of course she was truly terrified and panicked. The next night she had one of these terrible visitations again but this time it was interrupted by a beautiful man standing near her in bright white light and he said to her words of kind advice, "go to Michael's dad and he will remove this from you" or something like that.

So in the morning she found my son Michael and when she shared everything with him he told her, "my dad can remove this from you in 15 seconds." She was thrilled! How beautiful that there was a way of escape for her! But upon learning that I was a Christian, she became terrified in a different way, terrified of shame, of control and manipulation, and other things she thought of about "Christian people." The fear of shame was more profoundly dreadful to her than the fear of death and she did not have the courage to come to me.

I think that this dear sweet girl really misunderstood some things. Maybe her world view was shaped by some bad experiences with religious people. I think there were two things she missed. First, she did not have a place in her worldview that could believe just how *good the man in bright white actually is*, that he only has her best interests in mind, his motive is love without control, mercy without demand. Jesus would never send her to someone who was not at least a little bit like he is. So I think she had a basic misunderstanding of his true and sincere kindness. Secondly, and equally important, I think she somehow had Jesus mixed up for somebody else, she mistook him for a religious person.

In my experience, Jesus may be the most non-religious person anywhere. For him it's all about relationship. When Jesus looks fierce or demanding of righteous repentance, it is coming from a fierce, passionate, serious love. True love demands real justice because it fiercely defends people. That's Jesus. Jesus showed us heaven's culture by living it.

Now to the contrasting story, one of our friends dropped in at our house with a young woman who was having some serious trouble with some demonic stuff. She was deep in occult stuff also. I felt Jesus' real, intense and highly personal love for her and said some words on his behalf. Now most people would really love to hear these words but they really triggered something in her and she went stiff as a board, quite literally straight, and slid out of her chair under the table. She was twitching and her face was contorting and out of her mouth were coming some very strange sounding words. Our friend started shouting at the devil. I asked him to stop. I got on the floor next to her. I told the things in her to be silent and I spoke to the girl and said, "I know you have needed protection, I can see what happened to you (I gently mentioned something sad and specific here...), but Jesus is more kind than you have ever known and he can both heal you and protect you. He suffered with you when these things happened to you and wants to show you the truth." In a few moments Jesus showed her that he was really with her when bad things had happened, how deeply he cared, how he was willing and able to protect her at that time, and willing and powerful to protect her going forward. She put her head on my chest and I held her as she wept and wept. Then when she was ready, she, Jesus, and I together told the demons to leave her and never come back. There was no drama, only the sweet presence of Jesus.

David A. Melander

I am sharing all that because I think we have all misunderstood Jesus, just how genuinely good he is. And I think we mistakenly see him through filters of religion.

One thing Jesus certainly modeled was joy. How could he do that while being in the middle of the human pain and demonic "mud" all around him? The bible is very clear that he knew the hearts of men. That is a little like the guy who knows where every piece of stinky trash can be found in the "dump". When we read the gospels we see how Jesus often knew what people were thinking, or what was going on inside. That means he knew a lot of sad or ugly things that were happening. He understood why and how the people he loved were becoming so contorted in pain. So how did he keep himself in continual joy?

Jesus was extremely joyful because he could continuously hear and see Father's breathtakingly beautiful ideas and dream for people. He made his heart vulnerable to their pain and he did not need to shield his heart from it – he could be with the pain and simultaneously full of real joy because Father's beautiful dream was always greater and more real than their current condition, no matter how dark.

So I am hoping that we can look at our hearts and see if we are like Jesus or if he needs to help give us new hearts, to remove a heart of stone and religion. To do that I want us to take a look at the heart and intention of Father in the law and in realms of obedience. This flows from our understanding of the freedom experienced by sons and daughters. Learning this obedience in joyful freedom is part of what creation is waiting for (Rom 8:21: "...freedom of the glory of the children of God"). So this is actually important that we learn to live this as sons and daughters.

What we learn about his heart and his intention will free our hearts from what I call "a Heart of Stone and Religion".

- Ezekiel 11:19,20 "And I will give them one heart, and put a new spirit within them. And I will take the heart of stone out of their flesh and give them a heart of flesh, that they may walk in My statutes and keep My ordinances and do them. Then they will be My people, and I shall be their God"

Let's walk through this in several steps. We begin by looking first at Jesus' teaching on obedience, then at the heart of King David as he lived under the law, then at what God said about his most real intention in giving the law, and finally we return again to look at the words of Jesus.

What did Jesus teach us on obedience?
- John 14:15: "If you love Me, you will keep My commandments."
- John 14:21: "He who has My commandments and keeps them is the one who loves Me; and

he who loves Me will be loved by My Father, and I will love him and will disclose Myself to him."
- John 14:23: "Jesus answered and said to him, 'If anyone loves Me, he will keep My word; and My Father will love him, and We will come to him and make Our abode with him.'"
- John 15:10: "If you keep My commandments, you will abide in My love; just as I have kept My Father's commandments and abide in His love."
- John 15:14 "You are My friends if you do what I command you."

But I am afraid that somehow many of us read these verses completely wrong. We read these verses through a filter of religion that we bring to the text. Let's be clear about what Jesus is NOT saying:
- we earn love from Jesus and Father by obedience
- "if you *really* love me, you will get in line" in a form of shaming us to obey

That perspective cannot produce real obedience because real obedience flows from a joyful, relational cycle where you do something great together because you really want to. This obedience is really and truly entirely voluntary and performed for the reward of sheer joy.

Obedience without this relational joy gives no pleasure to Father God, it is dry as a morsel, empty, and it is useless in that it does not produce real kingdom results where LIFE is manifest in the obedience. That is why, for instance, Abba loves cheerful givers (2 Cor 9:6-7). Obedience motivated by sharing joy honors the character of God as Father. This is exactly what Jesus modeled continually for us, living in a virtuous cycle of joyous obedience because of the cycles of pleasure in love.

John Gill's commentary on John 14:21 is helpful[3]:
> Christ does not begin to love his people when they begin to love, and obey him; their love and obedience to him, spring from his love *to them*; which love of his towards them was from everlasting: but this phrase signs a clearer discovery of his love to them, which passeth knowledge; and some fresh mark and token of his affection for them; and which is explained in the next clause: and will manifest myself to him; not in a visible way, or in a corporeal form, as he did to his disciples after his resurrection; but in a spiritual manner, as when he makes himself known to his people in ordinances, and favours them with communion with him, and they see his beauty, his fulness, his grace and righteousness, his power, and his glory.

---

[3] see https://www.christianity.com/bible/commentary.php?com=gill&b=43&c=14

Here are the principles on which we understand the above verses:
1) The pre-existence of the love of Jesus to all people, and that of His Father who sent Jesus as an act of passionate and intentional love;
2) Obedience is not a condition of God's love but:
   a) Evidence that love has been written on a believer's heart. Growth for the believer does not occur by a focus on obedience but on developing genuine love, with obedience being simply an outward way to see the conversion of the heart toward love - and a further encouragement to grow in love;

   b) That the love of Jesus and Father is not in any way earned or made greater by obedience but that this love finds greater manifestation and greater connection to us in deeper obedience because it opens the windows and doors of our hearts.

Obedience creates a moment where channels of special receptivity to the Father's love are opened in the believer.

Barne's note on the Bible[4]:
"That true love to Jesus will produce obedience."

---
[4] see https://biblehub.com/commentaries/barnes/john/14.htm

Genuine love that captures the heart will certainly produce obedience. The love of Father and Son do not compel obedience but draw it out of the heart.

What King David Living Under the Law Modelled and What Father had Intended:

David stands apart from many in the Old Testament in how he understood the heart of God in the law and modelled the intention of God in how people were to relate to the Law.

David's relationship to the Law was joyful and relational. The law taught David to understand the heart of God and his ways. David reveals his relationship to the Law in Ps 119. It teaches him, aligns him, gives him insight into God's ways. "Oh how I love they law! I meditate on it all the day," (Ps119:97).

The Law clearly anticipated its own fulfillment in the coming of Christ while being a tutor to people, protecting them from many destructive consequences. Mostly, Father understood the evil one's intention to pull Israel into a trap that would kill them, to become a nation like those surrounding them, serving demons, knowing demons, carrying out deep and unnatural practices of witchcraft. That was not what Father wanted for them. Instead, Father was motivated to preserve them and to bring from them a savior for the world, in order for there to be a chance for mankind to be saved. This was not small stakes stuff. Every command in the Law was oriented around this critical principle: to preserve the opportunity for the savior of the world to come from Israel.

God was clearly self-sacrificing and served his people in the Law and serving his compassions for the future of mankind.

How Father made his relationship intention very clear in giving the law:

He reveals that his true intention in the law was relational, not legalism. I share a lot of verses here because I want you to really see the heart of relationship Father was seeking in giving the law. Read a few of these. I want you to see how truly important this was to Father:

- Deut 6:5 You shall **love the LORD** your God with all your heart and with all your soul and with all your might.
- Deut 11:1 You shall therefore **love the LORD your God**, and always keep His charge, His statutes, His ordinances, and His commandments.
- Deut 11:13 It shall come about, if you listen obediently to my commandments which I am commanding you today, to **love the LORD your God and to serve Him with all your heart and all your soul...**
- Deut 11:22 For if you are careful to keep all this commandment which I am commanding you to

do, **to love the LORD your God, to walk in all His ways and hold fast to Him...**
- Deut 13:3 you shall not listen to the words of that prophet or that dreamer of dreams; for the LORD your God is testing you to find out if **you love the LORD your God with all your heart and with all your soul**.
- Deut 19:9 if you carefully observe all this commandment which I command you today, **to love the LORD your God, and to walk in His ways always**—then you shall add three more cities for yourself, besides these three.
- Deut 30:6 Moreover the LORD your God will circumcise your heart and the heart of your descendants, **to love the LORD your God with all your heart and with all your soul**, so that you may live.
- Deut 30:16 ...in that I command you today to **love the LORD your God**, to walk in His ways and to keep His commandments and His statutes and His judgments, that you may live and multiply, and that the LORD your God may bless you in the land where you are entering to possess it.
- Joshua 22:5 Only be very careful to observe the commandment and the law which Moses the servant of the LORD commanded you, **to love the LORD your God** and walk in all His ways and keep His commandments and hold fast to Him

and serve Him with all your heart and with all your soul.
- Joshua 23:11 So take diligent heed to yourselves to **love the LORD your God**.

The intention of the law, at its core, begins in love, in relationship, it is "governed" by relationship, the heart to obey grows from relationship. Our problem is that the filter with which we look at the law was not ever the intention of God. Instead it is a filter created by generations who had rejected the heart of the law and who wanted to use the law to build a fortress of self-justification and self-righteousness. This continues to this day in religion.

Jesus' intention for us to learn obedience in relationship:
- John 14:15: If you love Me, you will keep My commandments.

What Jesus is saying in these verses on love and obedience are **not** measures by which we may be seen to fall so far short. Instead, these are profound promises of the results we will see in ourselves as we enter with Jesus into a cycle of love and joy with he and Father. It begins with a simple desire to be relationally connected with him, a hunger.

Jesus is telling us that real love from the heart manifests in obedience. That is, love naturally results in relational cycles of joy and obedience. However, if obedience is prime, it never results in love and we cannot use obedience to get love. Alternatively, love is enhanced in obedience in a virtuous cycle of joy as Jesus experienced and described his connection to Father. The joy cycle results in incredible promises of increased fellowship because acts of obedience that flow from love increase our capacity and ability to receive by opening the doors of our heart.

Removing a heart of stone and religion
- Ezekiel 11:19,20 "And I will give them one heart, and put a new spirit within them. And I will take the heart of stone out of their flesh and give them a heart of flesh, that they may walk in My statutes and keep My ordinances and do them. Then they will be My people, and I shall be their God"
- Eze 36:26, 27 "Moreover, I will give you a new heart and put a new spirit within you; and I will remove the heart of stone from your flesh and give you a heart of flesh. I will put My Spirit within you and cause you to walk in My statutes, and you will be careful to observe My ordinances"
- Jer 31:33, 34 "But this is the covenant which I will make with the house of Israel after those days," declares the LORD, "I will put My law within them and on their heart I will write it; and I will be their God, and they shall be My

> people. They will not teach again, each man his neighbor and each man his brother, saying, 'Know the LORD,' for they will all know Me, from the least of them to the greatest of them," declares the LORD, "for I will forgive their iniquity, and their sin I will remember no more."

If we are to manifest the freedom of the glory of the children of God that creation is longing to see, we need to be free from the hold of religion and have new hearts. That new heart lives and breathes in sonship. That heart learns to live from a motivation of a cycle of joy in relationship. That is of the essence of the culture of the country of heaven and what Jesus modeled for us. He is inviting us into this cycle of joy with he and Father and Holy Spirit.

Chapter 9

A Cleansing that Keeps our Love From Growing Cold

The revelation of sonship opens our eyes to live in the culture of heaven and to live with abandon toward it.

The joyful connection with have with the Trinity is the very thing that keeps our love from growing cold. It is a glowing hearth in our hearts, continuously fed with the fuel of seeing Father's eyes toward us and his joyful countenance.

This is important because Jesus said in Matt 24:9,10,12: "Then they will deliver you to tribulation, and will kill you, and you will be hated by all nations because of My name. At that time many will fall away and will betray one another and hate one another…. Because lawlessness is increased, most people's **love will grow cold.**"

Jesus wants us close to him. He can protect us and keep us through anything:
- John 10:29: "My Father, who has given them to Me, is greater than all; and no one is able to snatch them out of the Father's hand."
- 1 John 4:4: "You are from God, little children, and have overcome them; because greater is He who is in you than he who is in the world."

We are encouraged to be one who overcomes: (Rev 2:7; 2:17; 2:26-28; 3:5; 3:12; and 3:21):
- To him who overcomes, I will grant to eat of the tree of life which is in the Paradise of God.
- He who overcomes will not be hurt by the second death.
- To him who overcomes, to him I will give some of the hidden manna, and I will give him a white stone, and a new name written on the stone which no one knows but he who receives it.
- He who overcomes, and he who keeps My deeds until the end, to him i will give authority over the nations; and he shall rule them with a rod of iron, as the vessels of the potter are broken to pieces, as I also have received authority from My Father; and I will give him the morning star.
- He who overcomes will thus be clothed in white garments; and I will not erase his name from the book of life, and I will confess his name before My Father and before His angels

- He who overcomes, I will make him a pillar in the temple of My God, and he will not go out from it anymore; and I will write on him the name of My God, and the name of the city of My God, the new Jerusalem, which comes down out of heaven from My God, and My new name.
- He who overcomes, I will grant to him to sit down with Me on My throne, as I also overcame and sat down with My Father on His throne.

Now let's take a look at what is happening and what is coming quickly:

- 2 Thes 2:1 ff: Now we request you, brethren, with regard to the coming of our Lord Jesus Christ and our gathering together to Him, that you not be quickly shaken from your composure or be disturbed either by a spirit or a message or a letter as if from us, to the effect that the day of the Lord has come. Let no one in any way deceive you, for it will not come unless the apostasy comes first, and the man of lawlessness is revealed, the son of destruction, who opposes and exalts himself above every so-called god or object of worship, so that he takes his seat in the temple of God, displaying himself as being God. Do you not remember that while I was still with you, I was telling you these things? **And you know what restrains him now**, so that in his time he will be revealed.

> For the mystery of lawlessness is already at work; only he who now restrains will do so until he is taken out of the way.

Here are my comments on these verses:

First, Paul describes spiritual forces coming to deceive people. Second, we see that there is an angelic force withholding a demonic force that will be loosed which is involved in the falling away and the coming of the son of lawlessness. (We can see a similar type of event, the removing of an angelic force, in Rev 9:14). Importantly, we see that the "man of lawlessness" and the principle or activity of "lawlessness" is at the root of "love growing cold" in Matt 24:12

What we understand of the spirit of the times is found in these verses:
- 2 Tim 3:1-6: "But realize this, that in the last days difficult times will come. For men will be lovers of self, lovers of money, boastful, arrogant, revilers, disobedient to parents, ungrateful, unholy, unloving, irreconcilable, malicious gossips, without self-control, brutal, haters of good, treacherous, reckless, conceited, lovers of pleasure rather than lovers of God, holding to a form of godliness, although they have denied its power; Avoid such men as these."

- 1 Tim 4:1, 2: But the Spirit explicitly says that in later times some will fall away from the faith, paying attention to deceitful spirits and doctrines of demons, by means of the hypocrisy of liars seared in their own conscience as with a branding iron.

Most people see the current discordant world political climate to be very much what Paul is speaking about prophetically. Here is the "problem statement" we are dealing with: as these things come upon us, as "lawlessness is increased", how can we be people whose love does not grow cold?
- Matt 24:12 "Because lawlessness is increased, **most people's love will grow cold**."

2 Timothy 3 (quoted above). This passage describes the "spirit of the times" that we are now entering into. The dialogue will be harsh between all of us, particularly between generations. We must learn to move in the opposite spirit even while carefully speaking the truth. Although the times will be hard, the beauty of the presence of the Lord Jesus overshadows everything. Without any doubt, we would all rather go through hard times in the sheer joy of a living connection to Jesus than live in peaceful times without it.

Because of the nature of the discourse of this era, reacting in the "opposite spirit" is critical. Responding without defensiveness, responding humbly, responding while taking no offense. That is because we want not only to answer in truth but to walk in the truth by manifesting Jesus. We become "more than conquerors" because of the connection with have with Jesus and Abba.

How we respond is probably more important than what we say. Think of it this way, if Jesus had been "offendable", because he had the gift of seeing people's hearts (and often their thoughts), he could hardly minister the way he did. His ability to "overlook" so much of what was happening around him in favor of concentrating his direction on the beautiful thoughts of Father is what he modeled as our pioneer. We need to not only speak truth but to minister truth in the spirit and way of Jesus.

But because the public conversation these days is so dark, twisted, and just plain false, many believers are quite taken with a sense of urgency or ardency around the public discourse and are quite offended. This takes our eyes off of what Father is doing and saying around us. The political situation almost everywhere in the world right now is dark but when we respond in offense, we are really just manifesting the same spirit of the world. This is not living in kingdom culture – you can be "right" and yet not right.

Let's be clear. Scripture describes a coming time of persecution. These scriptures were partly fulfilled in the persecution of the early church under Rome but they have their strongest embodiment in the end of times con-joined to the "man of lawlessness" and the "falling away":

Scripture tells us that believers will suffer:
- Matt 24:13 and Matt 10:22 tell us that "the one who endures to the end, he will be saved". This verse indicates that endurance of believers is necessary during great stress of persecution.
- Matt 24:21,22: "For then there will be a great tribulation, such as has not occurred since the beginning of the world until now, nor ever will. Unless those days had been cut short, no life would have been saved; but for the sake of the elect those days will be cut short" (so, the elect are present during these very difficult times).
- Mat 10:17 – 22: "But beware of men, for they will hand you over to the courts and scourge you in their synagogues; and you will even be brought before governors and kings for My sake, as a testimony to them and to the Gentiles. But when they hand you over, do not worry about how or what you are to say; for it will be given you in that hour what you are to say. For it is not you who speak, but it is the Spirit of your Father who speaks in you. Brother will betray brother to death, and a father his child; and children will rise up against parents and cause them to be put to death. You will be hated by

all because of My name, but it is the one who has endured to the end who will be saved."
- Dan 7:21, 22: "I kept looking, and that horn was waging war with the saints and overpowering them until the Ancient of Days came and judgment was passed in favor of the saints of the Highest One, and the time arrived when the saints took possession of the kingdom."
- Dan 8:24, 25: "His power will be mighty, but not by his own power, and he will destroy to an extraordinary degree and prosper and perform his will; He will destroy mighty men and the holy people. And through his shrewdness He will cause deceit to succeed by his influence; And he will magnify himself in his heart, and he will destroy many while they are at ease. He will even oppose the Prince of princes, but he will be broken without human agency."

I believe that times of great victory are coming upon the church as well as times of difficulty. But in the sense that the presence of Jesus becomes wonderfully imminent, with great glory, there will be great joy and blessing even in the presence of difficulties.

How do we receive a cleansing that will keep our hearts from growing cold? The key is possibly found in these several verses that warn us of the powers that can divert our love from Father to things of the world:

- Rev 2:4 "But I have this against you, that you have left your first love" (so our love is the key…)
- James 4:4 "You adulteresses, do you not know that friendship with the world is hostility toward God? Therefore, whoever wishes to be a friend of the world makes himself an enemy of God."
- Ephesians 2:2 "that in times past they walked according to the course of this world, according to the prince of the power the air that even now works in the children of disobedience."

We are offered strength and cleansing:
- Luke 21:33-36 "Heaven and earth will pass away, but My words will not pass away. Be on guard, so that your hearts will not be weighted down with dissipation and drunkenness and the worries of life, and that day will not come on you suddenly like a trap; for it will come upon all those who dwell on the face of all the earth. But keep on the alert at all times, praying that you may have strength to escape all these things that are about to take place, and to stand before the Son of Man."
- Rom 12:2 asks us not to be conformed to this world's way of thinking but to be transformed, that is, to begin to see with heaven's eyes, from the culture of heaven.

The renewal of heart that protects us from all these things is having a pure and simple connection with Father in great joy:
- I John 2:15 "Do not love the world nor the things in the world. If anyone loves the world, the love of the Father is not in him."

The love of the Father contrasts here with the love of the world – they are mutually exclusive to each other. Why is the love of the Father a protection against the love of the world? How does this protect our hearts from growing cold? It is because we begin living from the values of another realm and our affections move us toward that realm.
- Col 3:2: "Set your mind on the things above, not on the things that are on earth."
- 1 Peter 1:13 "fix your hope completely on the grace to be brought to you at the revelation of Jesus Christ."
- 2 Thes 2:16 "Now may our Lord Jesus Christ Himself and God our Father, who has loved us and given us eternal comfort and good hope by grace, comfort and strengthen your hearts in every good work and word"

Therefore, we should set ourselves toward the aim of developing deeper affections for Jesus. We do this by receiving revelation that allows use to see: (a) all that he's done for us, and (b) his beauty, humility, compassion, fearlessness, strength. These together are like plows that deepen and soften the soil of our hearts and allow us to "melt" into passion. There is a mechanism built into the human heart for falling in love, designed by God, and I expect it's in our hearts because its part of God's own heart, being made in his image. That is, we love (a) what's beautiful; (b) what makes us feel safe, seen, treasured; and (c) when we feel that our needs are cared for. And of course, Jesus fits these like no one in the universe. And of course, you can say the same about Father and Holy Spirit because they share the same character and beauty.

Jesus is extraordinarily beautiful. Unredeemed human culture and religion may obscure that or dull our vision. But there has never been anyone so humble, so caring, such a servant, so joyful and radiant. When we really see him, it truly "wins our hearts" – and that is what we are talking about, the love that keeps our hearts from growing cold.

I remember watching our neighborhood parade a few years ago, standing on someone's lawn with one of my neighbors. We knew each other by name and she asked me "what are you learning in life these days". I started sharing about what I was seeing in Father. I shared some of the things I was seeing him doing and what I could see in him. She just melted. She literally said, "David you have won my heart" and I know she was seeing Father for the first time through me.

King David said "One thing have I asked of the LORD, that will I seek after: that I may dwell in the house of the LORD all the days of my life, to gaze upon the beauty of the LORD and to inquire in his temple" (Ps 27:4).

Now David was talking about his experiences in the real, heavenly temple because the "temple building" had not yet been built. He had seen the beauty of the Lord and was captured in wonder, fascination, desire.

I love what John Piper said[5], "Therefore, the beauty of God is as pervasive and practical as the glory of God. If we admire the glory of God, we are admiring God's beauty. If the glory of God has an effect in our lives, God's beauty is having an effect. If God acts to magnify this glory, he is acting to magnify his beauty."

There is a natural "cycle of love" you may say, that of:
- Love begins in discovery and wonder.
- When that love starts to capture us, we begin a process of "selecting" or "forsaking others", making a significant decision to exchange one love in favor of a greater love.
- Bonding. By this I mean that we let ourselves be truly touched in such a way that things actually change and rearrange inside us until our hearts are captivated and connected.

---

[5] see https://www.desiringgod.org/articles/how-pervasive-and-practical-is-the-beauty-of-god

- Maturing and becoming securely attached, confident we are loved, treasuring and protecting this love.

We need to be careful about religion, even things that have the appearance of being "good" or "morally centered" or things that we may even consider to be "Christian". This is important because however "true" we think our opinion may be, many of these things seem so right to us but are not truly of the *nature* of Jesus.

Frankly, it is very easy for us to be religious in contrast to having the heart of Jesus for people, especially around "moral" issues that are important. There is a "gravity" that pulls us toward building a life for ourselves that we can justify religiously, without being aware this is happening, one that is centered around our own sense of what is "Christian" or "right" but which is not flowing out of a relational connection to Jesus. We must therefore learn to make it our aim to live relationally with God, to focus on retaining a connection with him.

These days I am learning to pray like this:
> Father, reveal sonship to me. Let my whole being learn to agree with the Holy Spirit inside me to calling out, "Daddy, I need you" Rom 8:15 – 18. I see that as I learn sonship I learn freedom and strength and beauty;

> Jesus, let me see your beauty. Let me see your deep and romantic love for the church and everyone in it. Let me see your great heart, your bravery, strength, and safety, so that my heart can cling wholeheartedly to my first love. Rev 2:4;
>
> Holy Spirit, dear comforting friend, let me always learn to welcome and love your presence with me, to become soft to your leading, to let my heart learn to move with the movements of your heart. I love your humility, your servanthood, your constant comfort. Let me learn how to give you place to spread the love of God through all my heart (Rom 5:5)

I hope that you will join me in asking Father, Jesus, and Holy Spirit these things. It will make you secure in love in a way that your love will not grow cold when challenging things are upon us. Well, more importantly, it is purely for the fellowship of joy we'll share in heaven.

Chapter 10

Daniel and Joseph, God's Fame In The World, and The Anointing For Changing History

Creation is waiting for the revelation of the sons and daughters of God who will walk in his gift of joyful freedom. This is the moment in history where the time for this is so ripe.

In this section I am seeking to describe some of God's purposes in the nations of the earth and how his people fit into his desires. "As in heaven, so on earth". I believe that we can only do this as his sons and daughters, living in joyful connection and freedom. This is part of manifesting the culture of heaven on earth in creative solutions to impossible problems, in a true spirit of wisdom and revelation that we see in Daniel and Joseph.

Please accept here just a little bible lesson to begin. From my understanding, we see in scripture four cases for God's fame among the nations:

Case One:
General ways in which the Lord makes himself visible to the nations of the earth, "General Revelation":
1. Ps 19:1 – 6; Rom 1:18 – 20 "The heavens are telling of the glory of God; and their expanse is declaring the work of His hands" and "… because that which is known about God is evident within them; for God made it evident to them. For since the creation of the world His invisible attributes, His eternal power and divine nature, have been clearly seen, being understood through what has been made, so that they are without excuse".
2. Psalm 22:27 – "All the ends of the earth will remember and turn to the LORD, and all the families of the nations will bow down before him..."
3. Psalm 33:8 – "Let all the earth fear the Lord; let all the people of the world revere him."
4. Psalm 48:10 – "Like your name, O God, your praise reaches to the ends of the earth; your right hand is filled with righteousness."
5. Psalm 64:9 – "All mankind will fear; they will proclaim the works of God and ponder what he has done."

6. Psalm 98:3 – "He has remembered his love and his faithfulness to the house of Israel; all the ends of the earth have seen the salvation of our God."

Case Two:
God's fame extended through declaration to the nations and a mandate to people to spread his fame:
1. Psalm 96:3 – "Declare his glory among the nations, his marvelous deeds among all peoples."
2. Matt 28:18 – 20 – "And Jesus came up and spoke to them, saying, 'All authority has been given to Me in heaven and on earth. Go therefore and make disciples of all the nations, baptizing them in the name of the Father and the Son and the Holy Spirit, teaching them to observe all that I commanded you; and lo, I am with you always, even to the end of the age.'"

Case Three:
After the kingdom is established under Christ, and his church shares the fullness of his glory:
1. Daniel 7:14 – "He was given authority, glory and sovereign power; all peoples, nations and men of every language worshipped him. His dominion is an everlasting dominion that will not pass away, and his kingdom is one that will never be destroyed."

2. Isaiah 25:6; Isaiah 40:5; Isaiah 56:7; Isaiah 66:18; Isaiah 66:20; Isaiah 66:23; Jeremiah 3:17; Jeremiah 33:9; Ezekiel 39:21; Zephaniah 2:11 (many others)

But I want to pay special attention here to Case Four: Times and seasons where God acts in such a way that his activity is public, manifest, and visible such that it is a witness to the Nations:

1. David defeating Goliath, 1 Sam 17, "that all this assembly may know that the LORD does not deliver by sword or by spear; for the battle is the LORD'S and He will give you into our hands".
2. Exodus 9:16 – "But I have raised you up for this very purpose, that I might show you my power and that my name might be proclaimed in all the earth."
3. Joshua 4:24 – "He did this so that all the peoples of the earth might know that the hand of the LORD is powerful and so that you might always fear the LORD your God."
4. 1 Kings 8:43 – "...then hear from heaven, your dwelling place, and do whatever the foreigner asks of you, so that all the peoples of the earth may know your name and fear you, as do your own people Israel, and may know that this house I have built bears your Name."
5. 2 Chronicles 6:33 – "...then hear from heaven, your dwelling place, and do whatever the

foreigner asks of you, so that all the peoples of the earth may know your name and fear you, as do your own people Israel, and may know that this house I have built bears your Name."

6. 1 Kings 8:60 – "...so that all the peoples of the earth may know that the LORD is God and that there is no other."
7. Psalm 67:1 – 3, 7 – "God be gracious to us and bless us...that your ways may be known on earth, your salvation among all nations...God will bless us, and all the ends of the earth will fear him."
8. Psalm 102:15 – "The nations will fear the name of the LORD, all the kings of the earth will revere your glory." (as the Lord is compassionate on Israel)
9. Ezekiel 39:21 – "I will display my glory among the nations, and all the nations will see the punishment I inflict and the hand I lay upon them."
10. The God-appointed work of Daniel and Joseph, in worldly kingdoms, demonstrating his purpose of mercy through his activity through the world-powers of their day, is a clear example.

We normally look at history as a series of human events. However, there is an eternal story that is largely unseen, completely eclipsing the human story in power, breadth, and scope. The true and fundamentally underlying story is the history of Jesus' intervention in human history.

As we look at the world we now live in there is clear evidence that Jesus has consistently intervened in the course of world events, through obedient and courageous followers, to change its course and trajectory.

To walk through this together I want to begin with a brief review of the history focused on people who acted in radical obedience so as to change social, cultural, national, and governmental aspects of human spheres. Then we will look specifically at the anointing of Daniel and Joseph.

As we attempt to look at the interventions of Christ in our world and in its history, we may feel quite a bit of internal conflict between the glorious possibilities and the pain the world is now experiencing. I have a dear friend who often feels so badly that God doesn't just step in and fix everything. For example, we see the large masses of people who have no access to healthcare, who die or experience great loss from what would be easily treatable diseases – and this loss is juxtaposed against a history of the establishment of thousands of hospitals around the world, mostly by people who would tell stories of how God led them (or *commanded* them) to organize and build them. Along with that there are many thousands of believers who put themselves squarely in harm's way to provide healthcare. The tension lies in the intersection of *what is, what might have been, what may be*. For example, if believers had *not* built thousands of hospitals in poor cities around the world, how much worse might the situation be? And similarly, if more believers had been obedient to a call to serve, or that they had the needed courage or faith to be obedient, or that they had the support of those called to support them, we can imagine how these un-finished acts of obedience may have further helped mitigate the miseries we now see upon a devil-dominated world.

World culture, the world economic system, the political systems of the world are at a place that no one could have imagined. Who would have imagined that in this technological era that slavery would be at its apex? There are more slaves today than at any time in world history. The total number of slaves acquired in the entire ~300 year history of the trans-Atlantic slave trade (approximately 12 million persons) is much less than the number of current persons living in slavery today (approximately 37 million persons), not counting the hundreds of millions of persons in debt-bondage (approximately 150 million persons). Similarly, the number of persons who have died in wars and genocides ("rumors of wars") in the last century may be higher than *the total number of persons killed in war in all of human history **combined***. The number of persons now starving is 4 times higher *than the total world population* at the time our Savior told us about famine being a sign of the last time of world history. Much the same can be said of many aspects of human miseries – death and injury from earthquakes, violence from crime, domestic violence, and the like.

And at the same time, there is a grace being released in the world through Christ and by believers carrying profound vision and calling such as we could never even imagine. In fact, while we wear our earthly bodies, we are not capable to contain the glory contained in the accumulated simple stories Jesus will tell us about what his little brothers and sisters are now doing with his help. We could not contain the intensity of the beauty and glory of what he is doing in this moment on the earth.

Yet there is a path being cut right through the current evil age, a road on which there is love, health, healing, and redemption. And this path is not only the redemption of souls, it has resulted in enormous public benefits to mankind. This path has left a quiet impact on history's trajectory and it has been made by individual people who had the calling of God, who were given specific assignments from Jesus. This amounts to Jesus' intervention in human history.

History shows how God stands his people up in "kairos moments" in history to make these changes. That is, moments where history comes to moments

The Culture of Heaven And The Destiny of Peoples

where societies and cultures are in essence "ready for change".

The antislavery movement, a justice movement, came out of what Jesus did in the heart and life of people who could respond to him, in Olaudah Equiano, William Wilberforce, Clarkson, and William Pitt (Prime Minister) – 1780's in England. This same wisdom and divine leading was on Levi Coffin, Isaac T. Hopper and the Quakers. One hero to so many thousand is Harriet Tubman (Jesus specifically gave her direction and instructions in what she did). Think of her friend William Still (merchant and former slave), Susan B Anthony, Sojourner Truth (who adopted the name under clear direction from the Holy Spirit). The biographer of Sojourner Truth said, "...the force that brought her from the soul-murder of slavery into the authority of public advocacy was the power of the Holy Spirit. Her ability to call upon a supernatural power gave her a resource claimed by millions of black women and by disempowered people all over the world. Without a doubt, it was Truth's faith that transformed Isabella, domestic servant, into Sojourner Truth, a hero for three centuries at least[6]". Preacher Jarena Lee who spoke not only against slavery but as an early advocate for women's rights in the world. It did not end there. Consider Amy Carmichael rescuing hundreds of children from prostitution in India. Consider the *Not*

---

[6] See http://www.washingtonpost.com/wp-srv/style/longterm/books/chap1/sojournertruth.htm?noredirect=on

For Sale movement – David Battstone, Mark Wexler, et al. International Justice Mission's leadership, including Gary Haugen and his staff. All tell how they were called of God to this work.

It is not just recent history. This has been true since the church fathers. Consider for example the record of Telemachus who stood in the gladiatorial ring to renounce and oppose the violence before he was killed. And the emperor who learned of his obedience to conscience immediately stopped the practice.

John Witherspoon and many of the founders in America were radical Christian people with a vision of how a secular government could govern such as to promote liberty – to the effect of both establishing justice in the earth and of removing hindrance on preaching, Christian works, et al.

Consider David Brainard and others who stood for native rights against great opposition.

Chiune Sugihara, the Japanese Ambassador to Lithuania from late 1930's - delivered tens of thousands from death camps. He was a secret believer. He was awarded by Yadvashem as one of the "Righteous Among the Nations".

William Faraday, a Christian activist and scientist credited with critical discoveries in electricity and other areas of science that unlocked technological advances.

Frances Willard was an early suffragist and founder of the temperance union. Jeremy O'Hare (NoyOnlySundays.com) said about Francis Willard, "We don't associate women's rights with Christianity. That's a great shame because what historians call 'first wave feminism' wouldn't have existed had it not been for activist, evangelical women". Public health proponent, Frances's follower, Kate Shepherd, in New Zealand, was the first to win the right to vote for women. Like many justice movements in the earth, many people have forgotten that it was specific *direction and leading from Jesus himself* that were at the foundation of these movements. Of course, some have taken these movements down paths that their founders would be surprised at, but we can't discount the benefits the original founders were seeking as they were directed by God.

I think also of Christian Führer who was a renewal pastor in Leipzig, Germany, whose prayer meeting blossomed into a movement of over 300,000 people, leading to the overthrow of Communism and the reunification of Germany (our church in Minnesota had a tiny, little connection to this).

Norway's revivalist, Hans Nielsen Hauge, (ministry period 1790 – 1824) not only led in dynamic spiritual renewal but is credited by secular scholars with the "early industrialization" of Norway. He claimed that where he preached that the Lord would give him revelations of business plans and these plans led to great economic benefits to the regions in which he preached.

There are untold numbers of women who were led by God with record of specific instructions, visions, visitation, directives given to them. Florence Nightingale,

Evangeline Booth, Corrie Ten Boom, Lillias Trotter (an artist who had a strong call to evangelism in North Africa ca 1800), Jennifer Wisemen (leading the dialogue between Christians and Science – a famous astronomer). All of them received profound leading from the Holy Spirit as innovators in the space in which they moved.

Charlotte "Lottie" Moon, a missionary in China, helped stop foot binding and promoted rural health. Through her calls for justice she brought light to the gospel in high places, affecting the nation. Sun Yat-Sen had become a secret believer in Jesus while studying in Hawaii. His vision for a democratic, and economically prosperous China had great impact on China's history.

Rosa Parks and many US Civil Rights leaders were directed by God to speak for justice. Rosa Parks said, "I felt the Lord would give me the strength to endure whatever I had to face. God did away with all my fear... It was time for someone to stand up - or, in my case, sit down. I refused to move[7]."

Christ teachings, his mission, his assignments, and the leading of the Holy Spirit have led to:
- Rights for women (suffrage, et al)
- Rights for people of different races (both anti-slavery and Civil Rights)

---

[7] Quiet Strength: The Faith, the Hope and the Heart of a Woman Who Changed a Nation, Rosa Parks, 1994, Zondervan Publishing House

- The development of the limitations of powers and of "civil government"
- Programs to recover from addiction (many, including my wife's heritage)
- Education movements through history, from Gutenberg on up to Webster
- Broad availability of healthcare (most hospitals *worldwide*, at least prior to 1980's, had been established by people with specific calling and vision)
- Adoption and child protection programs
- Even protections for animals – the SPCA, the Society for the Prevention of Cruelty to Animals, was founded on scripture (Prov 12:10; Exodus 20:10; Exodus 23:4-5; and Jonah 4:11)

History records much of the biographical information of the founders of these movements, their testimonies of faith, how God lead them, how they understood their scriptural mandates, how they stood up against opposition with God's encouragement, etc. They changed history.

There is a greater release of this type of anointing on God's people going through the earth. His people can stand up with great courage especially as they have a revelation of their birthrights as sons and daughters. Abba's dear presence gives them strength to stand in difficult places.

Now I want to review what the bible teaches us from Daniel and Joseph because I believe this will be very helpful to form a picture in our mind of how this may be manifest in this generation. Here are some observations from Daniel and Joseph:

1. What God was doing was very public – with worldwide visibility – for the purpose that the love and mercy of God could be visible. God used them to provide a manifest and supernatural wisdom greater than others as a demonstration of the Lord, his sovereignty, his care for all peoples and nations.
2. These men were humble, obedient, willing to follow without measure of sacrifice.
3. The works brought in by their obedience were very beneficial to the nation even though they were not God-fearing nations. This is a great sign of God's mercy on all nations.
4. Both were interpreters of dreams and this was in an extraordinary measure such that they found favor from the kings.
5. Both Daniel and Joseph were people of great skill, people of wisdom from a divine source, of supernatural wisdom.
6. Both were in a WORLD system, not a "kingdom-system" and both were called to bring great benefits to these places. Consider that there is a calling whereby men and women of

God serve uniquely and strategically as instruments of God's purpose – in secular positions of influence within the seats of power of this world.
7. Consider Daniel in Babylon and that today we are in a Babylon-like economic system that covers much of the world. We have a mandate to bring supernatural benefits even within this system. And this begins with a mandate to pray for Babylonian economic systems. Jer 29:7 says, "Seek the welfare of the city where I have sent you into exile, and pray to the LORD on its behalf; for in its welfare you will have welfare." Even though we can see much of the cause of suffering and poverty in the current systems, we are called to seek its welfare in order to bring welfare of a higher order. This requires supernatural wisdom.
8. Daniel possessed a supernatural quality, a quality the Queen called "an excellent spirit" and "a spirit of the gods" wherein she recognized that Daniels wisdom came from God. See Dan 5:11,12 and 6:3.
9. The top world leader over Daniel, Nebuchadnezzar, recognized this same quality and it was not by intuition, it was by the clear, obvious, and public ways in which God intervened in the path of the country's history.
10. Similarly, our kingdoms and culture have specific problems that only divine wisdom

can solve. God is providing this supernatural wisdom to many. It is not an "ideological" or "theological" response to the world's problem, it is an answer growing right out of the cultures and systems that exist, wisdom given in the context of these cultures and systems. Wisdom from within Babylon, from within Egypt. Joseph did not get the dream, Pharaoh did. Joseph got *the problem* to solve by providing the interpretation to Pharaoh's dream from God. It was in essence and *invasion* of wisdom into culture.

11. Daniel had a group around him that were called to the same sphere of influence (Shadrach, Meshach, Abednego). We need to find community of people called to our mission.

Lance Wallnau said[8], "I am convinced that in the global community we have problems that can't be solved until the people that have supernatural abilities step on the scene." "What if those problems are actually indispensable to create a platform for the emergence of the next Daniel, the next Joseph, the next Esther." "What if God is visiting unsaved rulers with inspirations, desires, and visions, and dreams that they cannot fulfill until somebody of a supernatural quality of the Spirit of God is in proximity to them, located in their organization." "A whole new era of consultants,

---

[8] Quotes from Lance's brilliant message can be found on: https://www.youtube.com/watch?v=AiLLf04jkK4

educators, teachers, and trainers and problem solvers in every single area of the human dilemma emerging as a light in a dark place, being the head and not the tail because the blessing of Abraham might be releasing people of faith into every government, every system of the world to solves the problems that the world cannot solve without us."

What if the world is shaking so violently at this point in history in part so that the people with divine wisdom for solving problems can publicly emerge? What if the divine purposes evidenced in the scriptures above (Case Four) and in the example of Daniel and Joseph are intended to evidence God's mercy and presence, to affirm the authority and wisdom of Jesus among the nations?

I am experiencing this in my own life and I am welcoming everyone I know to be willing to allow the Lord to lead them in similar ways. What follows are some examples from my life.

Anti-Corruption:

For years I had an "inkling" that the Lord wanted me to engage in anti-corruption work. In 2018 he gave me a plan, a revelation which was a culmination of 3 years of holding these things before the Lord and waiting. The plan came to me as a "download" in great detail. Next Father said that I was to ask for a meeting with the President of the country to which the proposal was addressed. This took courage. The courage came from my Daddy being with me. I traveled to the country and met with a member of the President's staff and with the highest official in anti-corruption work. The meeting started badly because people were offended that an "outsider" would have the arrogance to write a proposal for them. I was grilled aggressively for two stressful hours. Then something wonderful happened because they could tell I was there for no reason other than love. Their hearts were won. Then they started to get excited because, well, there was evident wisdom in the plan, supernatural wisdom. They asked, "where did this come from?" because they knew it was remarkable, different, very wise. This project is still in process.

My hope is that this project will do two things. First, I hope and believe that Jesus will be glorified in this because his wisdom and goodness will shine through. Second, I know that Jesus loves the people of the world and if this project frees a major country, it has the potential to help as many as 1 billion persons, people who live in countries where corruption has a strong "brake" on economic justice and development.

A friend also told me that attacking corruption is a direct attack on human trafficking and many other issues. This is important work. Already I have been able to share the principles from the plan with persons from five countries working in anti-corruption work. In every case these people asked me where the plan came from, its source. They ask because the plan is remarkably redemptive and very original. I get to give the credit to Jesus.

Jesus is directing me in other strategic projects with great potential benefits and he is giving me supernatural wisdom to solve these problems. And I believe this is really something on Abba's heart now. So I will just ask you, would you be willing to let him take you in unexpected ways, in redemptive plans and purposes?

This is an important moment in world history and sons and daughters are being called to fill "princely" roles in the world. It does not require that we contain in ourselves the resources required but simply that we are willing to say "yes" to Abba. Certainly wisdom and favor are required. Open doors with Presidents and leaders won't open easily. But the Lord will open the doors.

The process I am recommending is this:
- Share Father's heart for countries, issues, and the people of the world. That means, being willing to enter into some measure of brokenness and humility. But it is a special privilege that Father gives to people who earn his trust by being willing to carry these concerns with him.
- Receive Father's mind on a matter and the direction and wisdom that come with that. It may be surprising or even "impossible" but let it sit with you and grow. For me it is normal that the time between receiving his heart and getting a clear revelation about what he wants

to do often occurs over several years. In every case the timing will be different.
- When you know the mind of God, and you have learned to articulate it to people, be bold and strong. Strength and confidence win favor.
- Be willing to serve and work hard with what the Lord gives you. Be ready to be sacrificial because this position pulls our hearts toward true north. It helps our hearts to avoid self-serving motives. Think of Jesus before going to the cross, putting on a towel and washing the feet of his friends.
- Be content to be used in either big or small ways. Starting small is beautiful. Jesus is after obedience for its own sake because of the relational connection it builds. Results will come, big or small.

We do not know what success may come, but our aim is obedience, not results. Perhaps most of all, our eyes are toward Abba's face, to see his delight and pleasure. We are seeking a kingdom and city not built by hands.

Chapter 11

Loving and Embracing All that He Loves

One time I was walking to my downtown bus stop. I was mentally tired from work and not in the greatest mood. In crossing the street I noticed a woman by my bus stop who in the inner reaches of my mind I thought to be extraordinarily "plain". In that, my inner thoughts were a kind of a judgement. And in the same instance I noticed *that Father noticed my thoughts*. I immediately tried to hide my thoughts or change the subject but then to "repent" almost in the form of an apology. I tried this quickly because I had a sense that he wanted to talk to me about my thoughts and I did not want to talk about it because I could immediately tell that Father had something to say and it was going to be serious.

But I knew I could not hide when he asked me if he could show me what he thought of this stranger and what was in his heart for her. I felt mildly resistant because I felt "I'm not that bad, am I?" But of course I knew inside that I desperately needed to hear him or I would never change, just be stuck in my own perspective, merely human. So he opened his mind to me and I could see how he made her in a very special and deliberate fashion because of the dreams he has for her. I could see a beautiful destiny. Then he showed me something that he *always* sees when he looks at people, her heart (1 Sam 16:7). Yes, Father actually looks at the heart. What Father was seeing was beautiful.

I could feel his encouragement as my wonderful counselor and yet I could feel a profound and fierce resistance to my way of thinking flowing from his hot and jealous love.

Now I know that the heart is deceitfully wicked (Jer 17:9). That's a fact. There is a lot of stuff in there that is distorting who we were made to be when Father planned us before the foundation of the world:

- Eph 1:3-6 "just as He chose us in Him before the foundation of the world, that we would be holy and blameless before Him. In love He predestined us to adoption as sons through Jesus Christ to Himself, according to the kind intention of His will, to the praise of the glory of His grace, which He freely bestowed on us in the Beloved.

- Matt 25:34 "Then the King will say to those on His right, 'Come, you who are blessed of My Father, inherit the kingdom prepared for you from the foundation of the world.

But he still sees his own beautiful image in us and the destiny he planned for each of us (see Eph 2:10 where he planned good works for each of us at the very beginning).

Think of this from the perspective of James 4:4 – 6: "You adulteresses, do you not know that friendship with the world is hostility toward God? Therefore whoever wishes to be a friend of the world makes himself an enemy of God. Or do you think that the Scripture speaks to no purpose: 'He jealously desires the Spirit which He has made to dwell in us'? But He gives a greater grace. Therefore it says, "God is opposed to the proud, but gives grace to the humble."

When we are thinking like the world, our thoughts are hostile toward God, they insistently pull in the opposite direction – and it leads to death. No wonder he is opposed to the world and its way of thinking. If you go around seeing people like the world sees them, you will act like the world. All the while, this woman was at the center of God's heart so much so that there is a beautiful, burning jealously of pure love going on in him.

To be clear, the jealously of God is not like jealousy we see in people. In God it is pure, giving, eager to bring people to destiny for their own sake. He is not controlling, manipulating, nor is there even a hint of self-serving in him. His jealousy is pure and it is a passion of love for all that we need to come into the beauty he so desires for us.

Rom 8:7 says much the same as James, "because the mind set on the flesh is hostile toward God; for it does not subject itself to the law of God, for it is not even able to do so" but the mind set on the Spirit is life and peace." That is, "thinking like God" or "thinking with God", or "having his mind" produces something wonderful.

It is OK that God is kind of offended by worldly thinking in us because he so longs for something better in us, something that can embrace the beauty he is creating in us and people he loves. And if we ever doubt that thinking like the world is "really all that bad?" just take a look at where it's gotten us.

In the experience I described above, I was a little offended by God at first, as if he wanted me to be perfect or something! Well, maybe he does. He wants perfect hearts. And its really not asking that much of us. If we are willing to share headspace with God he will be our champion, not our critic. His name is actually "comforter" or "counselor" (in fact, *wonderful counselor*). He wants us to succeed in this process. But sometimes he needs to plow up our human prejudice.

The reward of allowing him to plow through our human thoughts is wonderful: feeling clean and beautiful. We are indeed beautiful, especially after he messes with us. I am thinking it's a very good thing to be willing to exchange our opinions for his truth because it is a baptism in the culture of heaven.

One time I was hanging out at the lake home of some friends including an esteemed scientist. On the deck of a lazy, sunny afternoon, sitting aside a tall, cool lemon ice tea, Jesus surprised me with a question. He said, "what do you think about French people?" I knew instantly that although he was asking very humbly and sweetly that it was going to be serious business. I knew it was "bait" to something big. But I know Jesus enough to know that if it's important to him it will be very good for me, it would "save" me in a way. So I answered him and told him what I was thinking. Then he asked if I wanted to know what he thinks and when I said "yes" I was suddenly taken into another realm. I could see him dancing over France, over a hundred big and small places, he was joyful and calling out to everyone. I wanted to be like him because it was beautiful. And his beauty is not like a Hollywood image, it is a true beauty that radiates from everything he has inside himself. It is fantastic!

After that Jesus did not say much to me. He let it sit with me. But I found my heart changed. I started to love French culture and everything about France. And one thing I discovered is that Jesus is not just excited about the destiny of French people, but about all sorts of people, well, everyone.

Jesus is neither offended nor intimidated by people who are very "different", whether captured deep in occult things, or "liberals" or "conservatives", rich or poor, old or young, or "beautiful". These things matter to us a lot because we are invested in so many things of this present age. Jesus is already looking past this toward living with us in his own country and culture.

In 2 Cor 5:14-16 Paul says, "For the love of Christ controls us, having concluded this, that one died for all, therefore all died; and He died for all, so that they who live might no longer live for themselves, but for Him who died and rose again on their behalf. Therefore from now on we recognize no one according to the flesh; even though we have known Christ according to the flesh, yet now we know Him in this way no longer."

In this passage I understand Paul to say that since we have a new mind, and love controls us, we do not look at people outwardly any longer. Because we have the mind of Christ in both "mind" and "attitude" we see people from the heart. We see their destiny and intended beauty. We see the bride Christ sees.

James 2:1-3 talks about not seeing people for what they can do for us, not seeing people as rich and poor, but we look into eternity toward the wedding banquet, seeing their nameplate at Christ's table.

Isa 57:15 is one of my favorite passages:
"For thus says the high and exalted One
Who lives forever, whose name is Holy,

'I dwell on a high and holy place,
And also with the contrite and lowly of spirit
In order to revive the spirit of the lowly
And to revive the heart of the contrite'".

Living in the culture of heaven means trading our thoughts for the mind of Christ and learning the vocabulary of living in love. And this is a great exchange. Our old mind, even ways of thinking that we associate as "Christian thoughts" are often just human thoughts dressed in new clothing. The fresh, living and beautiful thoughts of Abba toward his children, of Jesus toward his bride, and of Holy Spirit toward his beloved must replace our thoughts.

We need a new mind about everything, about how we think about our jobs, our opportunities, our possessions, but nowhere is it as important as our thoughts toward people. They are centered at the heart of God. They are his dream. They are the prize sought by Calvary and the blood of Jesus.

The result we are seeking is truly beneficial to us in so many ways. The sense of being clean and beautiful is absurdly great. The sense of being like Abba is absurdly great. Do you remember how you felt intense joy when you did something for the first time and you saw your mother or father's bright shining face, beaming with pride? Of course, Abba's face is already beaming toward you, but somehow, when we try and be like him from the heart it blesses him even more. At the core, what he treasures most, is when our hearts become a little like his. Eph 5:1 says that because we are his beloved kids, we should try and learn to imitate our Father God by learning to walk in love, just as Christ also loved us.

Eph 5:1, 2, 10: "Therefore be imitators of God, as beloved children; and walk in love, just as Christ also loved you and gave Himself up for us, an offering and a sacrifice to God as a fragrant aroma...trying to learn what is pleasing to the Lord."

This is the core of living in the culture of heaven, it is of the essence of the shared thoughts of God, it is the grammar and vocabulary of heaven's language.

Afterword

I was flying home from an US East Coast with my son. I noticed spiritually that the stewardess was being pursued by something – something with the intent to kill her, a spiritual force that is sometimes involved when people have cancer. So I struck up a conversation with her, in 10 second snippets as she passed by for service. She said she was a proud cancer survivor. On the 4th or 5th round I asked her if we could find a time and place to pray for her. She agreed. When she came back the next time she said, "how about now?" I asked if I could put my hand on her arm and she gave me permission. Then I asked Father to touch her. She immediately collapsed but because that often happens when we pray for people, I had prepared by lifting the armrest of the seat opposite the aisle from me. I gently lowered her into the open seat. She was a little afraid. She showed me how the hairs on her arms were all standing on end and she said she could feel power going through her body. She wanted to know, "what *is* this!!??" I told her gently that this was Father's love removing any trace of cancer from her body. Then as peace embraced her she fell into a beautiful sleep as Father's power touched her. (Don't worry, she was only out for about 5 minutes and she didn't get into any trouble with her job).

That story may sound dramatic in a way, but I think that it was normal in several ways. First it is "normal" in that the church is growing into miracles as a way of life - a "New Testament" life. Second, it was normal in the sense that I *myself* did nothing but the ordinary. I was in fellowship with God. I was listening. I did what he I sensed him wanting to do. And if you put it that way, it is simple and possibly mundane, what we try and do every day. Most of the time what we see and sense Jesus doing manifests in more ordinary results but the "mechanics" of relating to him are the same in whatever way they manifest.

My goal in writing this book is to share the sense of desire Jesus has for his church in this time in history. Frankly, the fire-starter for this book was a word from a dear friend, an internationally recognized scientist in his field, saying that the Lord was asking me to write it. My motive in preparing this book is simply to be obedient, to open my heart to you, and share what I am learning. I hope that Jesus heart shines through every word.

For the last 30 years my wife Adri and I have been privileged to be part of a beautiful church. This church is a large Lutheran church that played an important part in introducing the charismatic renewal to many congregations around the world, Lutheran and non-Lutheran. People from this church were sent out to many congregations in various countries. I was privileged to be able to share the message of the beauty, power, and presence of the Holy Spirit with many through the International Renewal Center in a number of places. I know that in some small way we changed history.

We called what we were experiencing, "the Renewal". And by that we meant everything that came into the life of a congregation when the Holy Spirit's power and presence came in. And of course, when his presence entered people and their churches a lot happened, and a lot changed.

My heart for "the Renewal", one of deep passion and desire, is that it continue to grow deeper and deeper in all of us. Over the last several decades I have been seeking the Lord and seeking understanding from him as to what he really wants from us, what remains "undone" in this renewal, what he holds in his heart to give us and to receive from us. And over these years I feel that the insight has slowly grown. The messages in this book were shared as prophetic messages in the form of teachings I shared in my church. I am filled to the full with the sense that what I am sharing here is something that Jesus wants to say from his heart to us. My prayer is that every reader will be washed in the sweet heart of the living Lord Jesus, and his beautiful dreams and intentions will be fulfilled for each one of us.

That the Lamb may receive the full reward for his sufferings.

About the author

David Melander is married, a father to four children, and he lives with his family in Minnesota, in the USA. He has been engaged in ministry as a speaker and innovator for more than 35 years.

David is a businessman engaged in redemptive projects. He works in China, Indonesia, India and in many other countries. He has over 180 entry stamps into China alone. His work with an Indonesian bio-plastic maker won the company the World Economic Forum prize, Social Entrepreneur of the Year (2013). He is presently primarily focusing on Medical Devices, producing conferences and working in product innovation. He is targeting technologies that allow low cost, highly reliable diagnosis to become available to the billions of persons who are presently underserved with medical services.

Along with his work in business, he has been engaged in ministry for International Lutheran Renewal, serving churches with seminars on the power of the

David A. Melander

Holy Spirit in a number of countries. He also has been engaged in both anti-trafficking and anti-domestic violence work and serves on the board of several organizations in the field. He frequently speaks at Discipleship Training Schools for Youth With A Mission on the Father Heart of God and on the Gifts of the Holy Spirit, especially on using prophetic gifts like Jesus.